For past and present students
of Wycliffe Hall, Oxford

A Pocket Guide to Ethical Issues

Andrew Goddard

LION

The author asserts the moral right
to be identified as the author of this work

A Lion Book
an imprint of
Lion Hudson plc
Mayfield House, 256 Banbury Road,
Oxford OX2 7DH, England
www.lionhudson.com
ISBN 978 0 7459 5158 4
ISBN 0 7459 5158 9

First edition 2006
10 9 8 7 6 5 4 3 2 1 0

Acknowledgments
pp. 18, 19, 101, 116, 120, 121, 126, 128, 146, 171, 173, 176, 206 Scripture
quotations taken from the Holy Bible, New International Version,
copyright © 1973, 1978, 1984 International Bible Society. Used by
permission of Zondervan and Hodder & Stoughton Limited. All rights
reserved. The 'NIV' and 'New International Version' trademarks are
registered in the United States Patent and Trademark Office by
International Bible Society. Use of either trademark requires the
permission of International Bible Society. UK trademark no. 1448790.

A catalogue record for this book is available
from the British Library

Typeset in 10/13 Palatino Medium
Printed and bound in Malta

Contents

Acknowledgments

Many people have, in various ways over the years, equipped me to be able to write this book. A number have kindly read one or more chapters and offered feedback that saved me from embarrassing errors or poorer or unfair arguments – Dr David Clough, Revd Colin Coward, Dr John Goddard, Dr Simon Hettle and Dr Pete Moore. Any errors or weaknesses that remain are, of course, my responsibility and I am happy to hear about them from readers through my website – www.ajgoddard.net. I am particularly grateful to Morag Reeve and Catherine Giddings at Lion both for their remarkable patience and their encouragement and guidance as the book was written and prepared for publication. My wife Elisabeth and children Jonathan and Nell were also a great support as the book gestated and came to birth.

The book is dedicated with thanks to those who have studied at Wycliffe Hall where I have been teaching Christian Ethics for seven years. They have helped me in various ways to engage with these and other ethical issues, giving me new insights and perspectives and regularly challenging me to explain matters more clearly.

Introduction

Facing ethical challenges

We seem today to be bombarded with information and decisions that constantly raise ethical questions and dilemmas. Often these appear to be totally new and unprecedented. Even when the issues are not novel, fewer and fewer of us have received and accepted a philosophical or religious framework within which we are able to work out how to respond.

Sometimes we find we have to make such decisions for ourselves, and we are conscious that the path we choose can have major consequences for the sort of people we become and the sort of life we have to live. More often, we are aware of others wrestling with complex and challenging situations. They may be family, friends or colleagues. Increasingly, however, they are people who are not known to us personally but whose lives touch ours through the mass media. They may be characters in our favourite soap opera, or real people in real-life situations shown on the news who have to make decisions either for themselves or on behalf of others.

It is a fascinating exercise to stop and keep a record of the major ethical debates that we are encouraged to consider through our news bulletins and newspaper reports. In the course of a week towards the end of 2004, among the major moral questions that filled our airwaves were the following:

- A seriously ill baby approaching her first birthday lies in a hospital bed. Doctors believe they should not revive her if her breathing stops again. Her parents, however, believe she is a fighter and do not want to let her die. What should be done? Are doctors right to refuse to intervene medically?
- Is fox-hunting with hounds such a cruel sport that it should be made illegal or should we permit those who wish to continue hunting to do so under stricter regulations?
- Given that it is now generally accepted that Iraq did not have weapons of mass destruction, was it wrong to invade Iraq or does the fall of Saddam Hussein's regime offer sufficient justification for the war?
- Should governments do more than they are doing in order to combat the environmental problems caused by global warming even if it means a cut in their country's standard of living?
- Are a politician's personal and religious opinions on matters of morality sufficient grounds to reject him as a suitable candidate for political office?
- Should we restrict immigration into Britain?
- The daughter of an MP murdered by the IRA Brighton bomb has had meetings with the terrorist who planted the bomb that killed her father in the hope of understanding him better. Is this a response we should encourage among victims of violent crime?

The majority of these questions are, for most of us, 'academic' in the sense that we do not have to make the actual decisions ourselves. They are, however, issues on which we are often expected to have our own opinions. Probably everyone has strong views on at least one of these examples. Sometimes they will be well informed, sometimes more a matter of gut instinct or prejudice. Often, though, our honest response is one of confusion, uncertainty and ignorance. This is because we lack a coherent moral vision and so try to piece one together from the fragments of our responses to each moral dilemma. We can at least be thankful that – unlike doctors, politicians, victims of crime, and parents of very sick children – we are not faced directly with having to make the crucial decisions in such complex cases.

It would, however, be wrong to think we are totally at sea and reliant solely on the views and expertise of others. All of us are making ethical judgments all the time, even if we rarely stop to think about what we are doing or how we do it. Before reading any further and considering the specific issues dealt with in this book, it may be helpful to think through and draw up a short list of some of the major ethical issues that you have been made aware of in recent weeks. You will probably have your own strong views for at least one of these issues. Although we rarely do it, a crucial part of ethical thinking is to step back from our own views and ask a variety of questions of ourselves and of others involved in moral debates. It may be worth trying this for one of the subjects where you think you know what you believe.

- Why do you have the moral beliefs you do on the subject?
- What has shaped your opinions? It may be your upbringing, your experience, your expertise in the area, your religion or your gender.
- What reasons would you give to defend your views?
- What do you think is the strongest argument against your views and in support of a different perspective? How would you answer it?

In your list of recent ethical hot topics there will probably also be issues where you are less sure of what you think is right. Here it may be helpful to prepare for the discussions that follow in this book by thinking through what you might need to know in order to help you begin to make up your mind.

One of the main aims of this book is to provide you with an introductory guide to debates on a range of major contemporary ethical issues involving life, death, sex, violence, politics and society. Each chapter will provide some of the key facts that must be considered in these debates. For each subject, we will also explore the different arguments put forward by those with opposing views. The danger in an issue-by-issue approach, however, is that although we may end up with many of the pieces of the jigsaw, we still have little or no sense of the big picture.

Digging deeper

Most of us go through our lives rarely, if ever, having to face such major newsworthy ethical dilemmas. And yet all of us are also aware that at some point we may find ourselves no longer able simply to be armchair ethicists. We may suddenly find that we too face horrendously difficult moral choices in our own lives. When that happens, our responses will be shaped largely by the sort of people we have become through the much less monumental decisions we have made in the more commonplace situations of life. What will be decisive will not necessarily be our ethical expertise on the specific dilemma we are facing. Two other factors will probably be even more important: our deeper attitudes to more fundamental moral and spiritual questions (what we sometimes call our 'values') and the sort of character that we have developed (our virtues or our vices). Our outlook on life – what can be called our overall worldview – and the sort of person that we are will shape how we respond when big moral questions are no longer distant and 'academic' but painfully close, personal and real.

One of the important tasks, therefore, in thinking about ethics is to make connections between the issues, the ideas and arguments they raise, the sort of person we are and how we look at the world. One aspect of this is learning to dig below the immediate surface question. It is important to work out how specific, pressing moral dilemmas are related to wider issues, and to consider how we think about these deeper questions and respond to them even when we are not in a crisis situation. If we take the news stories we noted earlier, we can see that they make us consider a range of much more basic questions, questions that we may consider to be philosophical or religious. Any listing is obviously selective – part of the ethical debate is that different people will believe different, deeper issues to be at stake. But among the more fundamental moral questions raised by the earlier list are:

- How do I view death and the inevitability of the death of those I love?
- What do I think doctors can and should do to help those who are suffering?
- What limits do I think the law should place on human freedom? How willing am I for people to be allowed to do things that I personally find morally objectionable?
- Do I only get involved with others' conflicts when I think they threaten me personally or am I willing to take costly action to help others in need?
- How much do my own choices as a consumer show awareness of the effect of my actions on the environment?

- Can I and should I ignore my personal moral beliefs in my job?
- How do I respond to those who are different from me and whom I don't easily understand?
- What is my reaction to those who have hurt me?

Another important aim of this book is therefore to help you see some of the deeper layers in any moral issue. Hopefully it will become clearer how answers to particular ethical quandaries are linked to a much bigger picture – to a whole outlook on life. Responses to specific ethical issues need to be connected to our response to the big, broad ethical question, 'How shall we therefore live?'

By uncovering the hidden depths in one complex area of ethics we are also sometimes able to see connections between perhaps quite different questions. This can also help us to reach a more integrated understanding. We may, for example, spot tensions or inconsistencies in our own thinking or in the responses of others. It was suggested, for example, that a deeper question we need to think about in relation to fox-hunting is our view on the limits of the law and our freedom to do what others strongly consider to be immoral. This may then open up a much wider range of interesting, connected ethical questions. For example, is it coherent for me to campaign vigorously for a legal ban on hunting on the grounds of its cruelty while simultaneously objecting fundamentally (on the grounds that their proposal would violate some people's human rights) to those who seek to place stronger legal limits on abortion?

It may now be helpful to return to the ethical issue that you held strong views on and to begin digging more deeply:

- Does the subject raise more fundamental and wide-ranging questions about issues such as how we view life, death, suffering, relationships, love or freedom?
- How do your views on this ethical issue relate to your thinking on these deeper issues?
- In what ways do your views on these deeper issues shape your practical choices and attitudes in daily life?
- How might your response to these more fundamental issues shape your response to another 'hot' ethical debate?

This method of digging deeper may also help you begin to work out a personal response to an issue on which you are unsure of your views. By identifying one or two more basic questions that are linked to the issue and by working out what our choices and attitudes to these questions are in daily life, we can often begin at least to see the questions and concerns that should shape our decision on the issue.

Making moral decisions

We've already begun to explore some of what is involved in making moral decisions. Often introductions to the topic of ethics begin with a whole range of elaborate systems and technical terms and concepts, so that readers can work out whether they are – or wish to be – utilitarians, deontologists, consequentialists, intuitionists, naturalists, relativists, or some other species of ethicist. Rather than laying out all these stalls, it is perhaps more helpful to note four factors. Each person will understand these factors slightly differently and will give them varying weight in their judgments, but all of them shape how we make decisions about how to act.

The world in which we act

How do we view the world as a whole and the particular aspect of the reality of life that we face in this ethical decision? Part of this is covered by the process of 'digging deeper', but answering this question also requires us to understand how we think we should respond to parts of the world. So in relation to abortion we need to think about what an embryo is, and in relation to animal experimentation it is necessary to be clear what we think distinguishes animals from humans. Here we need expertise from various disciplines (for example biology or medicine), although this will not usually be sufficient for reaching an ethical conclusion.

The constraints under which we act

In making moral decisions we find that we are not totally unlimited. We are constrained by other people and other forces. These may be external constraints such as the law of the land that forbids certain actions or requires others. There may also be internal constraints, such as our conscience, which drive us to believe something is fundamentally wrong and must be opposed. These factors that tell us what ought to be done or not done are, of course, not absolutely fixed – we can repeal laws and educate our conscience – but they are part of what shapes our thinking. More controversial are appeals to constraints that are held to be universal and binding on all but which are not recognized by all. These may be appeals to natural law, divine command or some form of special revelation.

The ends for which we act

We act with purposes and intentions, goals and targets. We hope that, as a consequence of our actions, the world in which we act will be changed for the better. In making moral decisions it is therefore important to think about what we are intending to accomplish through any action. For example, by administering a drug to a suffering patient are we intending to kill them or to relieve their pain? By firing this missile in war are we seeking to attack enemy troops or to massacre civilians? One theme that will appear in the discussion of a number of subjects and which represents a significant division between different approaches to decision-making is whether the end itself ever justifies the means. Those who accept the consequentialist line of thinking will inevitably believe that it does. Others, however, will say that there are some situations in which, although the consequences of the action may be judged to be good (for example, an infertile couple enabled to have a child), the way this end is achieved is to be considered unethical.

The person who acts

Our actions not only change the world, they change who we are. We become a certain type of person as a result of the ethical decisions we take and act upon. What we do not only reveals something of the sort of person we are but also shapes the sort of person we are becoming. In recent years, there has been much renewed interest in the role of virtue and character in ethics. As none of us is an island, it is also possible to extend this way of thinking from a focus on the individual to the character of a community. In many areas of ethical contention, there are often concerns about the effects of certain actions on wider society and underlying differences about whether we want to become a particular sort of society.

Although these four elements of moral decision-making are

rarely explicit in our decision-making or in the chapters that follow, being aware of them can help us to reach our own conclusions and to understand areas of moral disagreement. Sometimes disputes will arise because people give a different weight to these factors. Often disagreements will be caused by different views of the world or by the fact that some feel constrained by factors (such as biblical commands) that others do not accept. Being aware of this can help us to unravel moral disagreements and discover their root causes.

Moving forwards

This pocket book clearly cannot be comprehensive. It does, however, seek to address many of the most important ethical issues we face at the start of the twenty-first century. They have been grouped into three main areas: beginning life, living together and ending life. This categorization is a reminder that ethics covers the whole of life and that major differences in ethical perspectives often ultimately arise out of different understandings of the meaning and purpose of human life, what it means to be human, and the nature of a good life.

The opening section examines a range of issues, such as reproductive technologies, embryo experiments and abortion, which focus on decisions concerning the start of human life. These are usually classed as 'medical ethics'. This is then followed by a discussion of issues that force us to think about how we live together as humans in community and in the wider world: war, punishment, our treatment of animals, the environment, asylum and immigration, sexual relationships, and poverty. The book draws to a close by looking at how we respond when life itself draws to a close, with a particular focus on the question of euthanasia. Although the book is probably best read by working through each chapter in turn, it has been designed so that each chapter can be read on its own. This makes it possible to look up and find out about one subject without having to read the other chapters. In a number of places, there are cross-references (in bold) to discussions in other chapters that may be relevant.

Although each chapter explores different viewpoints, this book cannot be neutral. It is important to realize that this is true of any guide book. For every person, what we personally believe to be important will inevitably shape even the way we introduce a subject. It is therefore important to be open about the fact that I write as a Christian. As a result, I hope that my way of understanding ethical issues and my own personal conclusions on particular subjects are shaped by the teaching of the Bible and the wisdom of Christians over the last two thousand years. I will, therefore, at different places refer to relevant parts of the Bible and the views of Christian churches. The chapters are, however, not explicitly structured around a distinctively Christian understanding, nor do they strongly defend one religious view against others. My own views will undoubtedly be clear on at least some issues, particularly in the chapters' conclusions, but the chapters make no assumptions about the reader. They aim simply to address questions that are of concern to those of any faith and to those of none; and to do so in a way that will help readers to reach their own conclusions.

1. Artificial Reproductive Technologies

Few things in life bring people more joy than the birth of their children. Few things in life can be more traumatic than wanting but failing to have a child of one's own. Throughout human history, infertility – the inability to bring forth new life – is a painful and, in many cultures, a shaming and humiliating experience. Although it rarely causes physical pain, the psychological scars are often deep. The significance attached to transmitting life is illustrated by the fact that the first divine command to humans found in the Jewish and Christian scriptures is 'Be fruitful and multiply' (Genesis 1:28).

Being unable to fulfil this command can lead people to desperate measures. This is confirmed by many stories in the rest of the Bible and by wider human experience across time and space. In ancient Israel we find the wives of the great patriarchs (such as Sarah and Rachel) developing a pattern of surrogacy in which slave women bear children on their behalf, often with disastrous results for family dynamics. There is the (to us bizarre) institution called Levirate marriage, which is laid down in Deuteronomy 25, recounted in the story of Boaz and Ruth (Ruth 4:10) and used as a challenge to Jesus in the gospels (Luke 20:27–33). Under this practice, if a man dies without producing an heir, his brother is to marry the widow and produce an heir for him! Both throughout history and in contemporary society there are cases of those who are unable to have children resorting to kidnapping – stealing another's child in order to meet their own lack. One such incident took place in the US in December 2004. A woman who had recently miscarried murdered Bobbie Jo Stinnett, who was heavily pregnant, and removed the foetus from her dead body so she could claim the baby as her own. This, it appears, was not unique, and a television documentary has already been made about the new phenomenon of 'foetus snatchers'.

More positively, societies may institute structures of adoption so that those who are unable to have children may receive and care for those children whose parents are unable to provide them with the necessary support.

These responses show the various forms of initiative that humans take in order to overcome the challenge of infertility. However, the Bible and other religious traditions also speak highly of those who simply turn to God, as the giver of life, and ask him to 'open their womb'. The classic Jewish example of this is Hannah, the barren wife of Elkanah. Elkanah's other wife had given him children, and she had then tormented Hannah because of her infertility. Hannah's prayer, born out of deep distress, is answered and 'in due time Hannah conceived and bore a son. She named him Samuel, for she said, "I have asked him of the Lord"' (1 Samuel 1:20). This reminds us of the deep mystery surrounding the appearance of new life. We experience new life as a gift and even usually non-religious people often speak of the 'miracle' of birth.

Faced with the pain of infertility the ethical challenge we are faced with is this: What are the legitimate means of human action by which – in order to enable the good gift of a new human life – we can intervene in the normal, natural process of procreation through sexual intercourse?

How to make babies: the biology and the techniques

We now know that the building blocks of new human life are male sperm cells and female egg cells, known as 'germ cells' or 'gametes'. Every one of these (and there are hundreds of thousands of them in each one of us) has a unique version of the human genome (see the chapter on genetics for further discussion of this science). This difference explains why even children of the same parents turn out to be so different from one another. For these gametes to begin to form a new life, 'conception' or 'fertilization' has to occur in which a sperm cell and egg cell join together to create a new cell (the 'zygote' or 'fertilized egg' or 'embryo'). The moral questions raised by artificial reproduction involving fertilization are discussed in the chapter on **in vitro fertilization** (IVF). Here the focus is on those forms of artificial reproductive technologies (ARTs) that do not produce an **embryo** but rather work with human sperm and eggs.

The techniques used in ARTs are necessary when infertility is caused by a problem in either the natural production or the delivery of the gametes. Human intervention seeks to overcome this problem by extracting sperm or eggs. The least controversial of these procedures and one of the earliest forms of assisting the development of new life is that of artificial insemination (AI). This is useful when the underlying problem leading to infertility is found to relate to the production or delivery of sperm, as sperm can be transferred into the woman's reproductive tract by artificial means (in other words, not through normal sexual intercourse). The earliest claim that human conception had occurred by this means was made back in 1790 and artificial insemination has now become standard practice in the field of animal husbandry.

A distinction has traditionally been drawn between two forms of AI. Even though they use exactly the same medical procedure almost all agree they raise significantly different moral questions. In some cases, the sperm is that of the husband. This is known as Artificial Insemination by the Husband (AIH) or 'homologous artificial insemination'. But another option is to use sperm from a donor – Artificial Insemination by Donor (DI) or 'heterologous artificial insemination'. The infamous first recorded case of DI was back in 1884, at Jefferson Medical College in Philadelphia. Dr William Pancost informed his class that he had discovered that the infertility of one of the couples he was treating was due to the husband being sterile. When he asked the students what he should do it was jokingly suggested that the best-looking student supply the sperm that was lacking! Dr Pancost took the suggestion more seriously than was perhaps intended and subsequently sedated the woman and inserted the sperm, despite claiming simply to be examining her. Nine months later, though she never knew it, the woman gave birth to the first child created by donor insemination. It was, however, only a quarter of a century later, in 1909, that the story became public knowledge and it wasn't until 1945 that the *British Medical Journal* carried a report on four cases of DI. This led to the first public debates on the procedure. A commission set up by the Archbishop of Canterbury called (unsuccessfully) for the procedure to be criminalized in England and in 1958 the Lambeth Conference of Anglican bishops said that it 'cannot see any possibility of its acceptance by Christian people'.

In both forms of artificial insemination any conception arises naturally within the mother's body using one of her eggs. But sometimes the problem is with the woman's eggs and here – as with sperm – someone may donate gametes to help an infertile couple. If both sperm and egg are accessible in the clinic it is possible to use a method that goes by the apt acronym of GIFT – Gamete Intrafallopian Transfer. Here, rather than simply inserting sperm, sperm and egg are mixed in the clinic and then transferred into the fallopian tubes before fertilization occurs. GIFT is distinguished from IVF (**in vitro fertilization**) because in IVF fertilization itself takes place outside the woman's body (from the Latin *in vitro* meaning 'in glass').

There is little doubt that those developing these techniques in recent decades have been driven at least in part by the desire to alleviate the human suffering that results from infertility. Of course, the desire for knowledge, prestige and financial reward are not wholly absent. Nevertheless, for many people the end result – enabling couples to have children they cannot have naturally – is sufficient justification for some if not all of these processes. On purely consequentialist moral reasoning it would appear that the good end could justify all these means. However, serious moral questions have also been raised. These need to be understood and assessed before artificial reproductive technologies using human gametes can be given a moral clean bill of health.

'Sex please, we're Catholics'

The common feature of all artificial reproductive technologies (ARTs) is that they bypass sexual intercourse between a man and a woman as the physical means of receiving the gift of new life. The first moral issue, which has made ARTs unacceptable in official Roman Catholic teaching, is whether it is *ever* right to use a means of producing human life other than natural sexual intercourse. The Vatican's *Instruction on Respect for Human Life in Its Origin and on the Dignity of Procreation* (commonly known as *Donum Vitae*) rejects all procedures that seek to produce human life outside the physical sexual union of husband and wife. It argues (as the Roman Catholic Church does in relation to contraception) that in God's purposes the sexual act has two goals and meanings that must not be separated. There is the 'unitive significance' of sexual union which bonds the couple together and the 'procreative meaning' of sexual activity shown in its openness to the gift of new life through such union. To seek one without the other – in this case to attempt procreation apart from bodily union – is to separate what God has joined together and is therefore wrong.

From this perspective, even artificial insemination using the husband's sperm to provide a child for a married couple who make love with each other but who are unable to conceive naturally, presents a problem, as it marks a move from a practice of procreation to one of reproduction. This is seen by some as the start of a 'slippery slope', which moves away from God's good ordering of human relationships and his means of providing new life. To seek the beginning of new life in the controlled procedure of artificial insemination is to shift pro-creation from the receiving of a gift through self-giving to the making of a product. Baby-making has moved out of the personal intimacy of the bedroom and into the technical world of the surgery. As with the official Vatican opposition to contraception, most Christians (including many Roman Catholics) are not persuaded of this argument. They would share a concern not to detach the creation of new life from marriage that includes physical consummation. However, they would argue that when physical consummation is incapable of yielding new life, AIH is a process that assists conception rather than artificially reproduces human life.

As soon as it is accepted that it is sometimes morally right to seek to conceive apart from sexual intercourse, we are faced with a wide range of ethical questions. These focus on how we are to view human gametes once we have removed them from the human body. What are we able to do with them as entities in their own right? They are now detached from the person whose genetic material they bear. Nevertheless, they still contain the potential for creating a new human being, a 'child' of the 'parent' whose sperm or egg is being used. Two questions require considerable thought: *Who* can use *whose* gametes? *Who* should know about the process? *What* should they know?

Husbands or partners? Dead or alive?

A central question is the relationship between the couple seeking a child and the source of the gametes used to produce a child. The old distinction between AIH and DI was the central one in a society in which there was a socially clearly defined and morally privileged category of 'husband'. In most societies today where ARTs are used to help infertility this is no longer the case. In the UK, for example, over 40 per cent of children are born outside of wedlock. As a result, most people would prefer to use the category of 'partner' rather than that of 'spouse'. Nevertheless, using the sperm of the husband is clearly the least morally problematic source. Any child will then be the biological offspring of a man and a woman who have made a lifelong and exclusive commitment to one another in marriage. (For further discussion of 'cohabitation' in relation to marriage see the chapter on **marriage and sex**.)

Even if it was argued that only the gametes of those who are married could be used, a further problem arises. Marriages end when a partner dies but gametes can survive beyond death, as sperm and eggs are often frozen and stored for future use. This development raises new possibilities. It has always been the case that some children never know their father because he died between their conception and their birth. It is, however, now possible for children to be conceived *after* the death of their father.

The famous case of Diane Blood brought this whole question to public attention. Her 30-year-old husband, Stephen, died after falling into a coma in February 1995. However, it was possible to take sperm from him and store it. Initially, Diane Blood was refused fertility treatment with her late husband's sperm in the UK, due to the fact that her husband's explicit consent for donation had not been granted. However, after a legal battle she was granted permission to travel abroad to receive such treatment. In December 1998 – over three years after her husband's death – she gave birth to her first son, Liam. In 2002 a second son was born, again using her dead husband's sperm. Finally, in 2003, UK law was changed to allow her to register her deceased husband as the posthumous father of her two boys. In Diane Blood's case the actual procedure used was IVF, but the ethical issues are raised as soon as one accepts the storage of human sperm or eggs.

On a purely emotional level, many people will respond to this possibility with a mix of delight and a sense of unease. There is the joy of a new child, fruit of the love of his parents, a sign that life is stronger than death. There is also, however, a new situation: children are being created to live in a single-parent family using the germ cells of someone who is dead and who never gave formal and explicit consent for his sperm to be taken and used to father children.

Eggs from embryos?

The question of consent and the implications of viewing genetic material apart from a person and their relationships become even more surreal in relation to female donation of eggs. One difficulty at present is the lack of eggs donated. (The procedure is much more invasive and unpleasant for women than men.) In the UK it is estimated that demand exceeds supply by a ratio of 200 to 1. As a result, scientists have begun exploring the possibility of harvesting eggs from the ovarian tissue of aborted female foetuses. Such ideas provoked widespread disgust and outrage when they were aired in 2003. A nightmare scenario was painted of a woman using the eggs from her aborted or miscarried foetus in order to become mother to a child who would in one sense be her granddaughter and whose real mother was never born. The procedure is currently illegal in the UK. However, unless other means are found to increase the supply of donated eggs, it is probably only a matter of time before this solution is accepted in some part of the world. Opposition to it may come to be viewed more in terms of an emotional 'yuk factor' than any serious moral thought. (After all, it does no physical harm to the already dead foetus and, as in the Diane Blood case, it could be seen as bringing hope and joy from a context of grief and despair.)

Gamete donation

It is generally recognized that there is a difference between the moral questions to be addressed when two people already in a relationship open to the gift of life decide to use their own sperm and egg to have a child, and when sperm or egg are donated. Can a couple use others' gametes to help overcome infertility?

Clearly once gametes are brought in from outside the couple there are real dangers of abuse. The first recorded case of DI described earlier is, arguably, most akin to rape. It also raises sharply serious questions about the extent to which ARTs are shaped by and perpetuate unjust relationships between men and women and risk making women into 'reproductive machines'. There have also been tragic cases of 'mix-ups' in fertility clinics when donor sperm has been used in error. One famous example of this was a court case in 2003 concerning who was the legal father of mixed-race twins born to a white couple as a result of the wrong sperm being used. Even more disconcerting is the infamous case of the American fertility doctor, Dr Cecil Jacobson. He gained the nickname 'the Sperminator' when he was sentenced to five years' imprisonment after fraudulently using his own sperm rather than that of donors to impregnate women. It is believed he became the father of up to 75 local children.

Perhaps the first question to be asked is how we are to think of what is happening in gamete donation. Is it simply a peculiar form of organ donation, raising no more moral questions than a kidney transplant from a stranger? Perhaps it is simply the earliest possible form of adoption? Or should we think of it more negatively? Is it to be viewed in a moral sense as a form of adultery, bringing a third party directly into one of the most intimate aspects of the marriage relationship?

It could be argued that gamete donation is a loving act to a neighbour in need. If someone is unable to have children and I can supply their need of sperm or eggs, what is wrong with doing so? Indeed, given the surplus of sperm and eggs most of us have, might there not be a duty to give out of that surplus to those who lack? Here we face the ethical challenge that there may be certain acts – perhaps even in some sense sacrificial acts – that we are able to do and which would bring delight and benefit to others, but which we nevertheless should not do. One example of this moral limitation (taken from the end of life) might be a terminally ill man's offer to donate his heart to someone in urgent need of a transplant even though this would end his own life. In the case of gamete donation, it could be argued that the natural ordering of family relationships and the fact that our germ cells are quite different from our organs place certain limits on what we are free to give to others in need. This is because of the life-giving, and to an extent identity-giving, powers of human gametes and because of the potentially damaging effects of donating them, for the individual who comes into existence, for the couple who receive them, and for wider society.

As soon as genetic material is introduced from outside a couple the question arises as to how the donor is to be selected. The traditional practice in relation to DI has been to encourage anonymity on the part of the donor but to allow those seeking insemination to know sufficient data about the donors to enable them to select a person so that there is some similarity (for example, in hair or eye colour) with the child's social father. Within the official processes, an anonymous record is also kept of all biological fathers. This is partly to prevent the realization of urban myths such as the man who finds he has married his own daughter, and to ensure that two people who know themselves to be children by donor insemination can check whether or not they share the same anonymous father. Some, however, might argue – perhaps citing biblical precedents in the use of household slaves as concubines or the practice of Levirate marriage – that it is better for donated gametes to come from someone known to the infertile couple, perhaps even someone biologically related to them. This latter case highlights most starkly the whole question of how the use of donated gametes automatically begins to restructure traditional family relationships: If the sperm donor is the social father's brother then he would be both the biological father and the uncle of the child.

Redesigning families

Leaving aside such extreme cases as the uncle who is really the father or the mother who is really the grandmother, by using sperm that is not from the husband, donor insemination creates two 'fathers' for any child. There is the social father who brings up the child within the family unit and the biological father whose genes the child carries. It is sometimes claimed that this is not as novel as it first appears. After all, a similar phenomenon occurs in adoption and with stepchildren: a child is brought up by parents other than their biological parents. There is, however, a difference between adoption and donor insemination (or use of donor eggs) which many consider highly significant. In adoption there is already an existing child whose biological parents are for some reason incapable of fulfilling their parental responsibilities. Another individual or a couple then stand in for those parents. They show love both to the natural parents and to the existing child by providing the care, nurture and stability that is needed but is lacking. In contrast, donor insemination intentionally creates a new human life for a couple by means of germ cells donated by another person. Indeed, there is the possibility that both sperm and egg may be donated, leading to four 'parents' for the resulting child – or even five if the birth mother is a surrogate mother who did not provide the egg and does not take the child as her own.

Even those who would not reject all such donation of gametes may conclude that there are limits that must be respected. The question is where these limits are to be placed and why, once we have begun to open up new possibilities, we place them where we do. There are three main categories of people who, as a result of gamete donation, may now be able to receive the gift of children that they would otherwise lack.

Single parents

It is now possible for a single person, particularly a single woman, to become a parent through the use of donated gametes. In January 2004, the head of the Human Fertilization and Embryology Authority called for a reconsideration of the law that spoke of the importance of a father, and in summer 2005 the UK government announced a major review of the law that would include this area. This opens up the whole question of whether everyone has a basic right to a child whether or not they are in any form of sexual relationship. If they do have such a right then there can be no objection to them producing a baby using donor gametes and, in the case of a man, the donor womb of a surrogate mother. If there is not a basic right then the question is under what conditions (marriage, loving relationship, same-sex or opposite-sex?) it would be acceptable for someone to be given and to make use of donor gametes in order to conceive.

Same-sex couples

There is now the possibility of a same-sex couple having children. This has been a reality for some time for lesbian couples who can relatively easily use donor insemination to produce a child. In April 2005 it was reported that this was being taken a stage further by Vicky Hill and Hayley Marlow who were planning to both be 'mother' to their child. Ms Hill wished to donate an egg to her partner that would be fertilized with donor sperm by IVF and then implanted in Ms Marlow's womb so that there would be a 'biological/genetic mother', a birth mother and a biological father, but no social father. A similar phenomenon is now happening among gay men. UK millionaires Barry Drewitt and Tony Barlow hit the headlines in 1999 when they become fathers to twins through a surrogate mother in the US and were both given the legal right to be named as parents. They had a third child in 2003 using the same egg donor but a different birth mother and are reportedly hoping for a fourth.

Senior citizens

In January 2005 it was announced that, after nine years of fertility treatment, Romanian Adriana Iliescu had given birth. The story was noteworthy because, at the age of 66, she was reckoned to be the oldest mother in the world, just breaking the previous record held by a 65-year-old Indian woman who gave birth to a boy after using an egg donated by her 26-year-old niece.

For some, such new opportunities created by these technological developments open Pandora's Box and represent a fundamental overturning of the natural, divinely created order. As such they are likely to prove damaging, psychologically and socially, to those children conceived in such situations. For others, however, these cases represent liberation from constraints that are experienced as restrictive and painful, and they provide a family and the joys of parenthood for those who would otherwise be unable to receive this gift.

Learning the facts of life

Whatever decisions are made about the morality of the various options now facing us as a result of donating gametes and procedures such as IVF, the further ethical questions that are raised are: Who should know what has been done in each individual case and what should they know about it? In particular, how much should any child be told when they inevitably ask, 'Mummy, Daddy where did I come from?'

Nobody, thankfully, knows the details of the exact circumstances in which they were conceived. There are many people alive, perhaps some reading this book, who were only born to their parents as a result of procedures involving donor gametes, but who are ignorant of this fact. It may have had no discernible impact on their personal identity and development.

In relation to DI, the traditional emphasis has always been on the anonymity of the donor both in relation to the parents and to any child born as a result. However, this is now being challenged and changed. The shift is largely due to the argument that to maintain anonymity on the part of the donor denies a person's basic human right to know their genetic, biological parents. As a result, in the UK, any children born as a result of sperm (or eggs or embryos) donated after April 2005 will now be able to access the identity of their donor when they reach the age of 18. This change in practice has raised some concerns that, even though donors are still not legally responsible in any way for those children born from the gift of their sperm, there will now be fewer donors. How many young medical students want their settled middle-aged family life disturbed in twenty years' time by a string of young teenagers wanting to get in touch with their 'Dad'? Especially if they have found themselves struggling to have children within their marriage.

If this change does lead to a cut in the supply of gametes then solutions to the problem of infertility that rely on gamete donation will become much more difficult, available to fewer people and probably more expensive. Many therefore argued against the change on the grounds that there was no absolute right to know one's biological parents and that to enshrine such in law would be to reduce the amount of good that can be done through ARTs using donor gametes.

Of course, whether or not the donor remains anonymous is irrelevant if the child is never informed that they were conceived by donor insemination. The fact that, in the UK, the social father and not the biological father is legally reckoned to be the father in cases of DI means that, if parents wish, the child may be kept totally in the dark about their origins.

A free market in eggs and sperm?

Finally, the phenomenon of gamete donation opens up a whole new series of moral dilemmas concerning the regulation of donation. Removing the biological means of reproduction from a person and storing and freezing eggs and sperm potentially creates a market in genetic material, supplied by donors. With infertility on the rise (as high a figure as 5 per cent of men are judged infertile in Western society), there is a very definite demand for the product.

Whether and how to control such a market is a major ethical challenge: Should donors be reimbursed? (For some time in the UK a paradoxical situation existed in which sperm donors were paid but egg donors – though they went through a much more complicated and painful procedure – were not.) Should there be a limit on how many children any one donor can father, and if so, how could such a limit be policed? Although you cannot trade gametes on eBay, the Internet is already a major resource for those seeking sperm or eggs, with sites such as www.mannotincluded.com and www.womannotincluded.com claiming 750,000 visitors a month.

There is also, even with gametes, the possibility of a form of 'designer baby' being encouraged. One infamous website advertises itself as providing the opportunity to bid on eggs from beautiful, healthy and intelligent women. By selling eggs for between $15,000 and $150,000, it claims to have had a turnover of $39.2 million in sales between 1999 and 2004. The nineteenth-century student response to Dr Pancost is now implemented via the Internet for big bucks, and once again the treatment of women is a major issue (though, to be fair, sperm is also offered for sale on a similar basis).

Conclusion

Roman Catholics and some others feared that the development of artificial insemination to help a husband and wife represented a 'slippery slope'. Whether or not this assessment is accepted, it is clear that simply by removing the building blocks of human life from human bodies – and hence isolating them from personal relationships and from bodily sexual intercourse – we have opened a Pandora's Box. The initial motives and intentions – to help those couples suffering from infertility – are highly commendable. The challenge is whether, and on what basis, one can place limits – moral or legal – on the use of gametes and artificial reproductive technologies. Experience suggests that human sperm and eggs easily become embraced by a culture that seeks to overcome natural limits in order to fulfil human desires through market exchanges. Children can then become less of a gift and more of a product or a project of the human will. The danger is that fundamental moral questions such as those discussed here are being ignored or that answers to them are being left purely as a matter of personal preference, with no social or legal norms or controls.

2. Embryos

'What if it were discovered foetal tissue was a delicacy; could you eat it?' These shocking words attributed to Christian theologian Stanley Hauerwas raise the question of what we think we can legitimately do with human embryos. In order to decide this it is first necessary to be clear what we think a human embryo is; and in order to reach some judgment on that it is necessary to understand the basic biology of embryo development. Only when we are clear on these matters is it possible to examine some of the current debates surrounding embryo experimentation.

What is an embryo? The facts of life

The embryo (or 'zygote' or 'fertilized egg') comes into existence when a sperm cell and egg cell join together at the end of the process of conception (or 'fertilization'). The significance of this event is one of the most contentious areas of ethical debate. Major ethical issues have developed in relation to embryos ever since, in 1968, it became possible to create human embryos in the laboratory and to allow them to develop through at least their initial stages under laboratory conditions.

Once fertilization has occurred the zygote begins to divide. By the third day it has reached sixteen cells, and individual cells start to differentiate into an outer layer of cells that will become the amniotic sac and an inner mass that forms the developing embryo. In pregnancy, to develop further, 'implantation' in the uterus must occur. This usually starts around the end of the first week after fertilization and is completed over the second week. It is only at this point that it is possible for the woman to know that she is pregnant.

Shortly after this stage – by about day fourteen or fifteen – what is called the 'primitive streak' begins to appear. This is an important developmental stage as the primitive streak is the precursor to the spinal cord and backbone. Its existence means that the separation of the embryo into twins ('twinning') is no longer possible.

Once this has occurred, rapid changes start to take place. By the end of week four, although the embryo is still less than one-quarter of an inch long, it has a beating heart and the brain has begun to develop.

Over the next month, the embryo becomes much more visibly human. It is during this stage that many prefer to use the term 'foetus' rather than embryo to mark the fact that from week nine all organs are present. Now almost all the major internal organs are in place, although many are not performing their adult function. By the twelfth week (the first trimester), all major internal organs are in place although not yet functioning. The foetus is also moving around, although it may not be until between 18 and 22 weeks that it is large enough for the mother to feel its kicks. This experience was traditionally referred to as 'quickening' and was given greater moral significance in the past before we had more detailed knowledge of foetal development.

Between weeks 24 and 26 the foetus reaches 'viability'. It has now developed functioning lungs, which would enable it – obviously with sufficient neo-natal support systems – to survive outside the womb. Also at this stage a functional cerebral cortex emerges and organized and measurable electrical activity appears in the brain. Ten weeks later, by week 35, the foetus, if born, is able to survive simply on milk.

The next great step is that of birth. As all who have experienced the imprecision of 'due dates' know, the exact date is also far from certain. The average time from conception to birth is 270 days (just under 39 weeks) but increasingly many babies are born premature (before 37 weeks in UK). Alex Franks, born in 1999 at 22 weeks, is the most premature baby in the UK to have survived, weighing just 1 lb 1 oz. In December 2004 Rumaisa Rahman, the lighter of two twins born at just 25 weeks 6 days, is reckoned to be the smallest baby to survive birth, weighing in at only 8.6 oz or 243 g.

Of course, birth and the first breath outside the womb is simply another stage, albeit a crucial one, in ongoing development. Although the public appearance of new life is legally decisive in most cultures today, many cultures have tolerated infanticide and do not attach such significance to birth. Some contemporary moral philosophers are also beginning to question whether we give too much importance to this stage in the process and need to reconsider our absolute ban on infanticide.

The moral status of human embryos

In making a judgment as to the moral status of the human embryo, the challenge is that there is clearly biologically a developmental continuum from the moment of conception through to birth and beyond. There is both continuity and discontinuity along this line, with some stages marking key biological advances. The moral significance of those developments is, however, highly contentious, especially given a fundamental continuity underlying the various stages of the process. Put simply, all of us who are alive can trace our existence back, through the changing scenes of life, to a fertilized egg that gradually became the helpless baby that has now become the person we are today. Does this mean that from the moment of conception a human embryo is to be treated with the same respect and accorded the same fundamental human rights as we would claim for ourselves as competent adults or for a newborn baby?

For Christians, the Bible gives some guidance here although its value is limited. After all, its concern is not with such questions and the biological understanding of its human authors was very primitive. The Psalmist, however, talks of God knitting us together in our mother's womb (Psalm 139:13–16) and the book of Job speaks of God's involvement in our formation before we were born (Job 10:8–12). We also read of God calling people before they were born, for example, the prophet Isaiah (Isaiah 49:1). Most significantly, Christians have also seen a clear sign of the full humanity of the embryo in the response of Elizabeth and John the Baptist (in her womb) to Mary and the embryonic Jesus she was carrying (Luke 1:39–44). Most Christians conclude from these biblical texts and from the wider biblical witness that they must treat the embryo as a human person from conception, someone (not *something*) made in the image of God according to Genesis 1 and thus worthy of full protection and respect. Others, however, are reticent about drawing so definite a conclusion from such texts. Clearly differences here will be decisive in determining how embryos are treated and so it is important to look at the scientific and moral arguments advanced for different viewpoints.

Conception?

Some argue that, even though we are speaking of a fertilized egg cell smaller than the full stop on this page, conception is the point at which we must recognize an embryo's full humanity. A central element of this claim is the fact that at conception a new and unique genetic identity is established that has a good chance of developing into a recognizably distinct and unique living human individual. It is clear that the embryo is alive (rather than dead) and human (rather than some other animal), so why should it be treated as less than human and its life not shown the respect given to other human lives?

While the embryo obviously lacks the qualities and abilities we associate with being human it has them in potential, as does a newborn baby or infant. Furthermore, as most of these distinctive qualities only arise much later in embryonic development and some (such as self-consciousness) are only present a considerable time after birth, we need to beware of making them essential for recognition of a human person. Finally, it is argued that, if there is evidence in favour of there being a human person present then, even if doubts remain, we should err on the side of caution and presume that we are dealing with a human neighbour. Thus, even those in the Christian tradition who gave a significant place to some later stage of development (what they called 'ensoulment', for example), argued almost unanimously in favour of protecting the life of the embryo at earlier stages in development.

This view is, however, not without its problems. Many, both Christians and non-Christians, have been wary of treating a human embryo from the moment of fertilization as if it were of equal moral standing to living and breathing human beings or to embryos at a later stage of development.

Post-conception?

The next stage after conception that is viewed by many to be of great significance is that of implantation in the womb, usually during the second week after conception. A number of reasons are given to justify treating the embryo differently before and after this stage in its development:

- At the earliest stages some of the cells will go on to form the embryo but some will go on to form the placenta – clearly not a human being – and these cells are not differentiated. It is even possible when there are only eight cells to remove one without affecting the normal development of the remaining seven. Only after four or five days does differentiation occur.

- An astonishingly high number of fertilized eggs fail to implant and so perish. The figures for this 'natural wastage' vary, with some claiming that as many as 70 per cent are lost before implantation and most accepting that at least 40 per cent probably die. Many find it hard to treat these deaths – unknown at such an early stage even to the mother – as the death of a human person.

- In pregnancy no relationship is established with the mother until implantation. Before that stage there are simply a small number of cells floating within the fallopian tube. It was impossible for writers in biblical times to think of a human life prior to it being knitted together in the mother's womb and so Christians cannot really appeal to biblical texts to argue for conception in preference to implantation as the decisive stage.

- During these early stages after conception it is possible for one embryo to divide and become two persons (identical twins), and even for two embryos to merge into one. This latter possibility may well go unnoticed, as in the case of a woman who only discovered she was what is technically known as a 'genetic mosaic' or 'chimera' when she needed a kidney transplant and found that neither of her children were suitable donors. It then transpired that she had been formed from four gametes (in other words, from the merging of two separately fertilized eggs at the earliest stages of development), with one twin's cells in her blood and the other twin's cells dominating in other tissues. If life begins at conception does this mean she is really two people?

To select 'implantation' as a crucial stage in embryonic development may be helpful in terms of natural pregnancy. It does not, however, directly help when embryos are being created in the laboratory. The questions are: To what stage should they be allowed to develop and how should they be treated by scientists? At present those who do not accept the 'conception' viewpoint tend to concentrate on the end of the second week and the formation of the primitive streak – the start of the nervous system and spinal cord – as the decisive stage. As with implantation, by this stage cells have differentiated into embryo and placenta and twinning is no longer possible. This stage is enshrined in British law as a result of the 1984 Warnock Report. Warnock claimed that this development at fourteen days marks the beginning of the *individual* development of the embryo, and her committee argued that no embryo experimentation was acceptable after that stage. It was also the point chosen in the US by the Embryo Research Panel of the National Institutes of Health, and reaffirmed by those on the President's Council on Bioethics who recently supported cloning for bio-medical research. Indeed, some today speak of a 'pre-embryo' as what exists at the earlier stages of development though it is generally recognized that this is more of a political and rhetorical device than an accepted biological distinction.

A gradual status?

Rather than trying to pinpoint a decisive stage in development either at conception or afterwards, some would argue that, just as there is a gradual biological development, so a graduated moral approach must be followed. The moral status of the embryo is enhanced as it grows because, as more of its potentiality is realized, it becomes more fully a human person. At each stage, exactly what treatment of the embryo is morally acceptable is thus a matter of debate and discernment. Some, such as Peter Singer, would go so far as to argue that even after birth we cannot always grant the full status of human person and inviolability of life, especially where there is some form of handicap.

Embryo experimentation

The status of the human embryo is an important issue in shaping responses within a number of ethical debates, including those surrounding **abortion**, **IVF** and cloning (for which see **genetics**). Here the focus is on whether human embryos are ever legitimate subjects of scientific experimentation. Such procedures are legal within certain limits in most Western countries although in Germany, in part because of its history under the Nazis, the 1990 Embryo Protection Act forbids the destructive use of human embryos.

For those who hold that human life is due full protection from conception, embryo experimentation is almost impossible to justify. There are well-established moral and legal principles concerning scientific and medical experimentation on human beings. At the heart of these is the requirement that free and informed consent is obtained from the person being experimented on. When the person is unable to give such consent (for example, if they are a child) then it is acceptable under certain conditions for consent to be given by someone else on their behalf.

Clearly an embryo cannot consent and so, if one accepts that embryos must from the earliest stages be treated in the same way as other humans, the question is whether anyone can give proxy consent for experimentation to take place. Although such proxy consent may be legitimate where the experiment brings some benefit to the person experimented on, most would reject allowing proxy consent where there is no benefit to the patient, particularly in cases where actual harm results or is highly likely. We would not, for example, believe it is right for a parent to let their child be experimented on when such experiments can bring no benefit to that child but would actually risk damaging them. This would be true even if the experiment may benefit someone else (even a sibling). The reason for this is that it would be to treat (or rather mistreat) the child as a means to some other end, seeking to benefit others while disregarding the child's own good.

Using this line of argument, if one is happy to accept the premise that embryos must be treated in the same way as children and other human beings who cannot consent, it is clear that experiments on embryos are morally unjustifiable. After all, the benefit of such experiments to others is unclear, they do not seek the good of the embryo, and in fact the experiment ends in the destruction of the embryo. In the words of the Vatican, 'To use a human embryo or the foetus as an object or instrument of experimentation is a crime against their dignity as human beings' (*Donum Vitae*).

If, however, the premise is not accepted – on the grounds that it is only some time after conception that the embryo merits being treated in the way we treat other human subjects of experimentation – then embryo research becomes a real possibility. There remains, however, the paradox that we are interested in experimenting on the embryo precisely because it is human. A new set of criteria is now needed to defend experiments on embryos as well as experiments on humans and **animals**. This is because the distinct status of the embryo, when seen as intermediate between that of humans and animals, demands a new way of thinking about experimentation.

When?

The first issue that needs to be determined is *when* an embryo ceases to be subject to the moral guidelines developed for embryo experiments and becomes considered sufficiently 'human' for experimentation to have to cease. Here the issues discussed in relation to the status of the human embryo are decisive. As noted earlier, the current prevailing consensus is that the appearance of the primitive streak at fourteen days is the crucial transition point. After fourteen days embryo experimentation is illegal in the UK (and in most other countries) and all embryos experimented on must be destroyed. Although now well established it is not impossible that this limit could be reviewed in the light of changing public opinion or evidence that experiments on later embryos may yield more beneficial results.

Why?

There also needs to be some justification provided for *why* experimentation on embryos should take place: What can and cannot be sought through such experiments? The primary moral grounds used to defend such experiments are those now enshrined in UK law as purposes for which embryo experiments may be 'necessary and desirable':

● promoting advances in the treatment of infertility;
● increasing knowledge about the causes of miscarriage or congenital disease;
● increasing knowledge about serious disease or the development of embryos or enabling such knowledge to be applied in developing treatments for serious disease;
● developing more effective contraception techniques;
● developing methods for detecting the presence of gene or chromosome abnormalities in embryos before implantation (see discussion under **IVF** and **genetics**).

Although potentially quite broad, clear limits are being placed here. In the UK the Human Fertilization and Embryology Authority (HFEA) which licences all such experiments carefully scrutinizes all proposed research projects involving human embryos. This is in an attempt to give some recognition to the special status of even the earliest stage of the human embryo while also seeking not to place excessive limits on the pursuit of scientific and medical research that could bring significant benefits to the fight against sickness and infertility. However, there has as yet been no major medical breakthrough as a result of embryo research, although experiments have led to the development and improvement of procedures for pre-implantation genetic diagnosis.

How?

Finally, questions have to be raised regarding *how* embryos are made available for experimentation. Initially the embryos available for experimentation were restricted to 'spare embryos' that were left unimplanted after being made during the process of **IVF**. Here written consent has to be given by the 'parents' for the use of such embryos in experiments. Some have defended the use of these embryos on the grounds that they would otherwise simply be destroyed. Experimentation at least offers the possibility that they may assist in medical progress prior to their destruction. In short, nothing is lost and something may be gained in such circumstances. More narrowly, others have argued that at least those embryos created by IVF that are damaged, and are either unable to come to full term or would be seriously handicapped if they did, are legitimate subjects of research.

More recently – especially in the face of the possible benefits claimed for stem-cell research (see **genetics**) – pressure has grown for the creation of embryos specifically for experimentation. This can be done using donor gametes to create embryos never intended for implantation or by cloning existing embryos. This has, however, raised further moral questions for some who are not opposed in principle to all embryo experimentation. This is because in this instance human embryos – unlike the 'spare embryos' from IVF – are being created with no intention that they could ever become babies but simply in order to be experimented on and destroyed. That is a development which some find unacceptable given their understanding of the status of the embryo and the respect due to it as a developing human life.

Conclusion

Until less than 40 years ago, human embryos only existed as a result of sexual intercourse. Except in the cases of miscarriage or abortion, an embryo was always something on the way to being born as a baby. We related to the embryo in and through the body of another human being who was pregnant and the many ethical issues raised were those concerning **abortion**. Now, however, we have extracted the embryo out of that context and nexus of relationships. As a result we have to decide how to treat it as an entity in its own right. We therefore have to determine its status as an object created by human will and totally under human control. It is clear that as yet there remains much disagreement about what status should be granted the human embryo in such a situation.

For some, perhaps the majority of contemporary Western society, the embryo has distinctive and unique features that distinguish it significantly from the rest of us, particularly in its earliest stages of development. While worthy of respect it is not at all times and in all places to be accorded the full dignity or 'rights' we grant to fellow human beings. If that is the case, then we may be justified in using the embryo in ways that we believe will bring benefit to others, even if this requires its destruction. For others, however, the embryo can and must only be treated as we would treat any other fellow member of the human race. For most Christians, particularly, the call to care for the weakest in society and the fact that God became a helpless embryo in Mary's womb means we must see and treat every embryo as a fellow human made in the image of God. In that light, to use an embryo as a means to our own ends, particularly when it is still far from clear what benefit is gained by so doing, marks a frightening disregard for the good of a weak and powerless human neighbour.

3. In Vitro Fertilization

Until the late twentieth century, human 'conception' or 'fertilization' – when a sperm cell and egg cell join together to form a new cell (the 'zygote' or 'fertilized egg' or 'embryo') – had never been witnessed by human eyes. It was part of the mystery of the gift of new life that occurred hidden inside the woman's body when one of the millions of sperm cells released during sexual intercourse met an egg cell (released every month or so in 'ovulation') in the fallopian tube and fused with it. All that changed in 1968 when scientists Robert Edwards and Barry Bavister, having brought this process about outside the human body, witnessed and photographed what took place. They succeeded in fertilizing a human egg in their laboratory and the process soon became known as *in vitro* fertilization or IVF for short.

Just as there is a long wait from conception to birth in the natural course of events so there was a long wait – over nine years rather than nine months – before the first live birth by IVF took place. On 25 July 1978, Louise Brown was born and was hailed as the first 'test-tube baby'. Since then over one million children have been born by this process around the world, children who would not exist without the pioneering research of Robert Edwards, Barry Bavister and Patrick Steptoe. And yet major ethical questions are still raised about the process of IVF and its implications.

As a process, IVF could be organized in such a manner that relatively few people would raise ethical objections. If the

gametes of a husband and wife were used to produce an embryo
that was then implanted in the wife, in the hope that it would
come to full term, it would merit little discussion in a book on
ethics. True, the sexual act has been bypassed and conception
has been accomplished by human technique in a laboratory and
these may be important developments, but otherwise there are
no great novelties to cause concern. The reality of IVF, however,
is somewhat different and three major areas of controversy arise.

Donation of egg or sperm cells

The gametes used in fertilization may not belong to the husband
and wife but may instead be donated by another party or parties.
This raises a whole series of questions that begins with earlier,
more primitive forms of artificial reproduction such as artificial
insemination. Issues such as the redesigning of family structure
and who should know what about the donation of egg or sperm
cells were discussed more fully in the chapter on **artificial
reproductive technologies**, but they also apply to IVF.

Status of the embryo

What distinguishes IVF from more primitive forms of ART is
that it results in the creation of a fertilized egg or a human
embryo. It is therefore necessary to make a judgment about the
status of this embryo from the moment of conception and
through the various stages of its development. The confusion,
even doublethink, that exists in relation to this difficult moral
question of the status of the human embryo is illustrated by the
tragic case of the Del Zio family, who in 1973 (five years before
Louise Brown) almost became the first ever parents of a test-
tube baby. Sperm and egg from the couple were mixed in a flask
at Columbia Presbyterian hospital with a view to IVF and

implantation. However, the Chief of Obstetrics discovered this and, because the experiment had not been approved and he personally feared any baby produced by such means would be a 'monster', he opened the flask and destroyed the culture. Doris del Zio was clear about what this amounted to: 'As far as I was concerned at that time he had murdered my baby... As far as I was concerned that was my child.' The same sense of the continuity between the earliest fertilized egg *in vitro* and the final child was memorably portrayed in the comedy *Friends* when Phoebe talked to the embryos about to be transferred to her womb. It is clear that for some people, at least some of the time in the process of IVF, embryos (even at the earliest stages) are humans. In other times and other places they are simply a collection of cells. The question of 'spare embryos' which is specifically related to IVF is discussed in this chapter, but the wider biological and ethical issues surrounding the human embryo were more fully covered in the chapter on **embryos**.

Embyro selection

Because we are dealing with human embryos and can examine their genetic make-up, it is now possible to select embryos prior to implantation in order to create a baby that has certain characteristics.

'Spare embryos'

In theory it is, of course, quite possible to develop a programme of IVF that simply creates the number of embryos required for implantation and then lets nature take its course. This would mean fertilizing no more than three (and probably only two) eggs at a time. This is because, although miscarriage of at least one embryo is likely after implantation, using more than three would be a high risk. In the UK, over half the babies born as a result of fertility treatment are twins or triplets. As a result, in 2004 new regulations limited the number of embryos to be transferred to two if the woman was under forty and to three if she was over forty. To fertilize only the number of embryos to be transferred is clearly an inefficient method of proceeding. The costs – both financial and emotional – of IVF are so great that such a limited procedure is rarely used in practice. Instead, a larger number of embryos – around eight is probably the norm – are created in the first cycle of treatment. Those that are not transferred become 'spare embryos' which are then frozen and preserved for the future. It is reckoned that at least a quarter of a million embryos have been frozen in Britain since 1990 and over time the numbers in storage have increased from just over 50,000 in March 1999 to over 116,000 by March 2003. This raises a major moral dilemma: What is to be done with such 'spare embryos'?

Make another baby

The first and least controversial response is for the embryos to be used later by the couple from which they came. This can happen should their IVF treatment fail (success rates for live birth from a single IVF course are not much better than for choosing the right number on the throw of a die), or should they wish to have further children in the future. Although there is some evidence that using frozen embryos presents more risks to the mother during pregnancy and perhaps to the children born, this response at least intends that the embryo be brought to birth and cared for by its two parents.

Even this solution is not without its potential problems.

Marriages and other relationships do not last for ever and this can lead to even more heart-breaking moral dilemmas. In 2002, Natallie Evans began a court case (which has now been taken to the European Court of Human Rights) to try and claim her six frozen embryos. They had been created the previous year using the sperm of her then partner. The relationship had subsequently come to an end and he had withdrawn his consent for use of the embryos. As her ovaries had been removed the embryos were, in her words, 'my only chance to have a baby'. The courts ruled, however, that under UK law the embryos could not be used without her former partner's consent and they would therefore have to be destroyed. Lorraine Hadley, another woman caught in a similar predicament, in her case after divorce, vividly summed up her perception of what was happening: 'An embryo is not a possession to be divided up in the divorce proceedings. It is a baby in the making. I fully accept that men have rights too. But I find it abhorrent that we should be able to create these little human beings – and then flush them down the toilet on a whim. Why should one of us have the right to say the embryos should be destroyed simply because it doesn't suit them any more?'

Adopt an embryo

Another response to spare embryos is to donate them to another couple. Here a case genuinely could be made that this simply extends the charitable act of adoption further back into the earliest stages of human life. An organization called 'Snowflakes' encourages such embryo adoption and there has even been some intriguing debate among ethicists as to whether it would be legitimate for Roman Catholic nuns to rescue embryos destined for destruction by offering to carry them to term! The reality, however, is that embryo donation is not a common decision, perhaps because the parents would find it strange for one of their children to be born to other parents. There is also little demand for donated embryos, perhaps because most parents want a child that is 'theirs'. In 2001, out of 25,000 IVF treatment cycles, only 189 used donated embryos and although over 70,000 children have been born in Britain by IVF (about 1 per cent of children born are now IVF babies), less than 2,000 of these have been from donated embryos. The 'adoption' solution can, however, create its own ethical conundrums, particularly where the embryos are orphans. The challenges were most evident following the case of Marion and Elsa Rios, two Americans who received IVF treatment in Australia in 1981. When they died two years later in an aeroplane accident the frozen embryos potentially became heirs to their great fortune. There was a rush of offers to adopt these particular embryos – a rush that rapidly subsided when it was ruled that the embryos could not inherit their late parents' wealth even if brought to full term!

Destroy the embryos

The default option is simply for the frozen embryos to be destroyed. Under UK law this is the automatic fate of embryos after five years unless the 'parents' give written permission for continued freezing. In 1996, 3,000 embryos were destroyed under this legislation.

Experimentation

A final option is for the embryos to be donated for medical research. This means that they will be experimented on in the hope that such study will increase human understanding and perhaps enable development of more effective techniques for combating infertility, or even (through stem cell research – see **genetics**) help find cures for some diseases. Since the Warnock Report in the UK it has been legal to experiment on embryos until they are fourteen days old and then they must be destroyed. For those who view the human embryo as morally equivalent to any human being this is an outrageous violation of traditional medical ethics. The one subjected to experimentation is clearly unable to consent, gains no benefit from the experiment, and is finally destroyed at the end of the procedure. Some, however, defend such practice not only on the grounds that a distinction must be made between the early stages of embryonic life and later stages but also on the basis that if the embryo has no chance of further development and is destined to be destroyed then perhaps by experimentation some good can be gained from this situation. Some of these ethical issues were discussed more fully in the chapter on **embryos**.

Designer babies?

The creation of more embryos than is needed by the parents creates a further new issue: On what basis is a selection made concerning which embryo(s) to transfer to the mother's womb? If there are eight embryos to choose from, how should the two to be implanted be selected? It could of course be done randomly and in ignorance, but for many that is both irresponsible and risky. Selection can be done on a much more orderly, reasoned basis, which considers the unique features of each embryo and the desires and needs of the parents or wider family. This takes place through 'pre-implantation genetic testing' and immediately raises the spectre of a 'designer baby', a process by which parents choose their preferred child from among the range of embryos created, much as they might choose their favourite wallpaper for their dining room.

In fact, the reality at present is more related to the desire to avoid having sick children. Embryos can be screened when there is a known risk that they may have a significant genetic defect. This is to ensure that those transferred to the mother are not affected. Such pre-implantation genetic diagnosis (PGD) was used for 21 live births in the UK in 2002. It can obviously be used not just by those who are infertile but also by those who are able to have children naturally but are concerned that natural conception might yield a severely disabled child. The question is, 'What are acceptable grounds on which to screen?' Even when these grounds are limited to medical conditions controversy remains (at the end of 2004 a licence was granted to screen for an inherited form of bowel cancer), and pressure is likely to mount for social criteria to be included, most obviously the selection of the child's sex.

Despite its goal of creating a healthy child, ethical questions have been raised not only about the inevitable destruction of the embryos judged to be 'flawed' but also about the implications of such practices on attitudes to the disabled in society. While at present this procedure is relatively rare, some have asked if there is a danger that it could become so commonly accepted that it will one day be considered irresponsible for parents not to 'select' between embryos if there is a known risk that they may pass on a serious disability.

Recently this has developed a stage further with the acceptance, in certain cases, of pre-implantation genetic screening (PGS). In 2003, Tom Ballantyne-Roberts became the first child in Britain to be born after genetic screening of embryos even though there was no history of genetic disorders in his family from which he needed protection. In his case, his mother had had twelve unsuccessful cycles of IVF treatment and his embryo was selected after the embryos were subjected to a simple test for genetic abnormalities in order to discover which was most likely to come to term as a healthy child.

Also controversial is the creation of a 'saviour sibling' in order to help an existing sick child. In April 2003, the Court of Appeal heard the case of the Hashmi family whose four-year-old son, Zain, was suffering from the rare blood disorder thalassaemia, and as a result he required a bone marrow transplant. Overturning an earlier court decision, it ruled that his parents could create embryos by IVF and screen them to find the one able to provide the necessary match for such a transplant. Although they have not yet been successful in bringing a 'saviour sibling' pregnancy to term, they and other parents are now in theory able to select and implant an embryo 'designed' to provide matching tissue or blood cells to enable an existing child to receive treatment. From a purely consequentialist perspective, such a procedure would appear highly commendable. It does no physical harm to the embryo selected (though of course other embryos will be created and never brought to term), and it offers real hope of healing – in some cases from a fatal disease – to the existing child. It does, however, make the very existence of the new child dependent on satisfying certain conditions. It could therefore suggest or imply that their identity and value is to be found not in who they are but in what they are able to do for their elder sibling.

For some this is the most blatant example of a danger implicit in all ARTs – the commodification of children so they become products in a consumer society. It is also, for many, the start of a 'downwards spiral' towards more and more selection criteria becoming acceptable. From that perspective, as more and more knowledge about the genetic make-up of embryos is gained, the pressure for 'designer babies' through pre-implantation genetic diagnosis and screening will increase. Sex selection is already permissible in the UK but only when it can be justified on medical grounds. Requests are, however, already made on other grounds (for example, producing balance in the family), and the new review of legislation is open to allowing greater freedom of choice in these matters. In societies where the emphasis in most areas of life is on personal freedom to choose according to one's own preferences, judgment as to what would be selected and what would be rejected will also vary enormously. The major concern is obviously that such selection will be used to eliminate unusual traits and to seek to 'normalize' future generations. The complexity of the issues and the different value judgments that might be brought into play is evident from the fact that there have already been reports that some deaf parents or parents with dwarfism are seeking to use such techniques to ensure they are able to produce deaf or dwarf children.

Conclusion

In the case of IVF, the ethical challenges that have already been raised in relation to earlier artificial reproductive technologies are combined with those relating to how we treat embryos. While some carefully controlled forms of IVF may raise little or no serious moral difficulties except for traditional Roman Catholics, the reality of how IVF is practised is much more complex and presents an ethical minefield. There is the personal challenge faced by an infertile couple eager to have children: 'What forms of IVF are we morally happy to use?' More significant perhaps are the wider and deeper ramifications of this technology for society and the way we think about the beginning of life and even what it means to be human. IVF both reflects, and in turn perhaps helps to encourage, a changing popular perception of the experience of having children. For most of human history, having a baby was something that was largely outside our control. As a result many viewed it as a gift, perhaps from God, perhaps from nature. The only question was how to come to terms with the gift one was given or with the fact that one did not receive this gift. Today such an attitude is increasingly rare. We have greater (though still fairly limited) control over 'baby-making' and so children can become viewed not as a gift but as a right. There is also the real and increasing possibility of significant choice and control over the characteristics of our children. Although this holds out the promise of being able to prevent great suffering it also runs the danger of being captured by a consumerist approach. Children could then come to be viewed effectively as a means, even a product, to fulfil parental desires. Particularly in pluralist societies where moral consensus is hard to achieve and even harder to enforce by law, the momentum – as perhaps shown by the recent plans to review UK legislation – is likely to be towards the sovereignty of individual choice, with fewer legally and socially defined limits and norms because of a lack of shared moral vision.

4. Abortion

'I'm pregnant!' These words can convey a whole range of human emotions, from ecstasy after years of unsuccessful 'trying', to shock, horror and fear at the implications of carrying a new life or revealing an illicit sexual relationship. Whatever the reaction, we can be certain that the speaker is a woman not a man. We can also be sure that although pregnancy was not something under the woman's control and may have come as a surprise, neither did it happen (unlike many illnesses) without any warning whatsoever. Its origins can be traced back to some recent prior experience, usually willed. We can also be confident that, as a result of being pregnant, the woman's own body and health will be affected in the coming months and, if all proceeds smoothly, she will – within a relatively short space of time – find herself responsible as a mother for the care and nurture of a new, helpless human being. The moral question is whether it is acceptable to take action in such circumstances to bring the pregnancy to an end by means of abortion, and if so, when.

History

Abortion, unlike many other ethical issues raised at the start of life (see earlier chapters on **artificial reproductive technologies**, **IVF** and **embryos**), has been a medical and a moral issue for thousands of years. Unwanted pregnancies are almost as old as the human race. Down through the ages people have sought various means to bring pregnancy to an end, and this has led to ethical debates about the procedures. The worlds of ancient Greece and Rome were very familiar with abortion, using various forms of herbal medication and surgical intervention in an attempt to bring an end to the developing life in the womb. Moral reactions to it varied. Aristotle and Plato were supportive in certain situations but the famous Hippocratic Oath (written in the fourth century BC) historically taken by doctors included the promise, 'I will not give to a woman a pessary to cause abortion.' The early Christians were marked out by their opposition to abortion and to infanticide, which was also common in the ancient world.

In large part because of the influence of Christian opposition, the Western world historically tended to place severe limits on abortion. This attitude began to change in the 1960s and, as a result of legislative changes, abortion became much more easily available and common. In the UK the decisive shift came with the 1967 Abortion Act, while in the US it was the landmark 1973 decision of the Supreme Court in the case of *Roe vs Wade* that led to changes. The effect of these changes on the frequency of abortion has been very significant. In the early to mid 1960s there were about 15,000 to 20,000 legal abortions a year in the UK and (although figures must be tentative) it is reckoned there may have been a similar number of illegal abortions. There are now about ten times that many legal abortions (roughly 185,000) each year in the UK and about 1.3 million each year in the US, with the number of abortions happening annually in both countries now approaching one-third of the number of annual live births. It has therefore been said that the most dangerous place for a human being to live in these countries is within its mother's womb.

Thinking about pregnancy

Much ethical debate about abortion focuses almost exclusively on the status of the **embryo**. This is clearly an important part of any moral argument and will be discussed later, but it is also important to consider what different approaches to abortion say about how we view and respond to pregnancy.

For some, pregnancy is almost understood in terms of an assault on the bodily integrity of the mother. At times in the abortion debate appeals are made on the basis of a woman's rights over her own body. In a famous article on abortion, the philosopher Judith Jarvis Thomson sought to argue that, even if it is accepted that the embryo is a person with a right to life, this does not mean that abortion is always wrong. To defend this position she carries out a thought experiment in which you imagine you have been kidnapped by a Society of Music Lovers. You wake up to find they have hooked you up to an unconscious violinist who is dependent on using your kidneys for the next nine months or else he will die. Her argument is that even if he has a right to life (which now depends on you allowing yourself to be restricted and used in this way), that does not make it wrong for you to detach yourself and refuse to allow him use of your kidneys for this period. In short, his right to life does not oblige you to provide the necessary bodily support to maintain that life in a way that overrides your right to bodily independence. You can detach yourself without violating his right to life and, by analogy, the pregnant woman can do the same to the foetus without this being a violation of any right to life that it possesses. While this analogy may be applicable if pregnancy occurs as a result of rape, it is more difficult to sustain when pregnancy – which is after all a much more common, natural and relationally based human experience than being kidnapped in your sleep and attached to a sick violinist – is the result of consensual sexual intercourse.

The violinist illustration also represents an attitude that views pregnancy as fundamentally a parasitic relationship. While there is one sense in which there is some truth in this – the embryo/foetus is dependent on the mother and lives off her body to grow – to reduce pregnancy to this or to make it the primary model for understanding pregnancy forgets much of great importance. This is, after all, the natural method of human generation by which every one of us came into the world. The womb is not being misused when it hosts a fertilized egg that then grows into a child. Furthermore, the relationship between the woman and the embryo/foetus cannot be reduced simply to a biological one. It is one that involves emotions and, ideally, a loving relationship of nurture and dependence in which human bonds are established and new life received.

Another option is to view pregnancy as an illness for which abortion is the medical cure. Again, there is an element of truth in this as pregnancy risks some damage to the mother's health. Under British law the ground for almost all abortions is that 'the continuation of the pregnancy would involve risk, greater than if the pregnancy were terminated, of injury to the physical or mental health of the pregnant woman' (Clause C of the Abortion Act). In reality this enables something very close to abortion on demand up to week 24. This is because the risk of continuing almost all pregnancies could be argued to be greater than the risks of termination (assuming terminations themselves do not cause longer-term psychological or other health problems – a view which many question). The fact that there is a risk of damage does not, however, mean that pregnancy should itself be viewed as an illness (perhaps a form of sexually transmitted disease?). Many activities and experiences carry potential health risks but that does not mean they are treated as illnesses. Most pregnancies are not viewed in terms of illness and doctors are usually asked for advice on how the mother can continue in good health and protect the health of the embryo/foetus rather than for the 'cure' of abortion.

In various ways, each of these understandings of pregnancy tends to view its continuation as what has been called by some a 'good Samaritan act'. By maintaining a pregnancy the woman goes beyond what she is obliged to do and, even though it is costly to her, meets someone else's needs. Abortion is therefore not in any sense a violation of someone's rights although, interestingly, the allusion to Jesus' parable implies that abortion would be a failure to love one's neighbour.

In contrast to each of these more negative understandings is the view that pregnancy is fundamentally positive and good. This standpoint sees pregnancy as the natural, divinely ordained means of receiving the good gift of human life and learning to love a totally new neighbour. Though not without its pains and dangers, which in some situations are very great, it is inherently something that should be welcomed. Pregnancy is rarely a wholly positive experience – receiving new life is not a matter of our choice or ultimately under our control and it always brings restrictions and challenges. It is, however, something we should learn to receive with thanksgiving and wonder rather than reject or view in fundamentally negative terms.

In reality, of course, every pregnancy is unique both in terms of objective context and subjective experience. One important question, however, is whether the meaning and significance of any pregnancy should be determined by the decision of the pregnant woman, or whether there is a moral reality here that we either choose to respect and come to terms with or to reject and deny. However psychologically realistic, is it morally coherent to view one pregnancy in one way – perhaps largely negatively and so to consider an abortion – and to give another pregnancy a quite different, more positive status? The language of 'every child a wanted child' is used in various ways in the abortion debate. Such an attitude can, in relation to pregnancy, suggest that it is ultimately the desire and emotional reaction of the mother – 'Do I want this child?' – that determines the status of the pregnancy. If that is the case then it becomes almost impossible to discuss the ethics of abortion, as the meaning and moral significance of every pregnancy is decided by the pregnant woman whose interpretation and wishes have become primary.

The human embryo

If a pregnancy is experienced and viewed primarily from one of the more negative standpoints then abortion might appear to be relatively unproblematic. It may even be seen fundamentally as a positive (even if regrettable) remedy to a difficulty – the ending of a bodily assault, the removal of a parasite, the curing of an illness. The challenge is that for at least some stages, perhaps all stages, of the pregnancy many people believe that such an account does not consider the whole truth. In particular, it fails to take into account the reality of the embryo/foetus that is removed and destroyed as part of the process.

Drawing the line

As discussed in more detail in the chapter on **embryos**, there is much debate about the status of the embryo as it develops from the single cell created by the fusion of sperm and egg into the baby born about nine months later. Those who are willing to consider infanticide will obviously have no fundamental problem with abortion at any stage. However, most people wish to find a moral position that maintains the prohibition on killing a baby after birth but permits abortion during at least some stages of pregnancy. To do this requires the drawing of a line in the process of the embryo's development somewhere between conception and birth. Before that line is crossed in pregnancy it is considered permissible to abort and kill the embryo (which is classed perhaps as a 'potential person' rather than a 'person'). After that line has been crossed, however, abortion (except possibly in exceptional circumstances) becomes wrong and is morally equivalent to infanticide. The big question then becomes where to draw that line and why it is drawn there.

Absolute prohibition

For some people, especially many Christians, there is no 'before the line', as the line is to be placed at the moment of conception. This is when pregnancy, or more precisely, fertilization strictly begins, as a new unique human being gains their genetic identity and begins their development. From that moment the developing embryo is thought to deserve the same respect and to hold the same right to life as any other human being. Christians who hold this view appeal not only to the scientific evidence of what happens at fertilization but also to biblical texts that speak of God's involvement in human life in the womb (see **embryos**).

It is important to realize that this understanding is not only opposed to all abortion. It is also, if it is consistent, opposed to some common forms of 'contraception'. If a form of contraception potentially prevents the implantation of a fertilized egg (rather than the fertilization of an egg), then on this understanding it must be considered to be a very early abortion. This means that, strictly speaking, all intra-uterine devices (IUDs, the 'coil'), certain forms of the 'pill', and the 'morning-after pill' are to be considered not as forms of contraception (even though they sometimes do work by preventing conception) but as abortive treatments.

Pre-implantation 'abortion'

Many women – including many Christian women – in good conscience use forms of contraception that potentially prevent the implantation of an already fertilized egg. This is one factor that (along with the medical evidence discussed in the chapter on **embryos**) gives support to those who believe that a line should be drawn later – but not much later – than fertilization. Intervention at this early stage – prior to implantation at the beginning of the second week – is legitimate, and if it is held that 'pregnancy' only begins at implantation when a relationship is established with the mother then this is not strictly a 'termination of pregnancy'.

In most countries, experimentation on embryos is prohibited after the appearance of the primitive streak or after fourteen days. There are clearly questions as to why an embryo in the laboratory can only be experimented on up to this stage and then has to be destroyed while an embryo in the womb can be destroyed at a much later stage in its development. The apparent inconsistency could of course be resolved either by effectively banning abortions or by considering experimentation up to a later stage of development.

Once one moves beyond these two decisive stages of fertilization and implantation there is much greater continuity in development. It therefore becomes far more difficult to draw a line in a clear place and to argue that status can fundamentally change once the line has been crossed. There are, however, a number of possible places where this line could be drawn.

Sentient being

For some, abortion becomes problematic when the embryo is able to feel pain. There is, however, much dispute over when this becomes a reality and in what sense the embryo can be said to feel pain. From as early as seven weeks there is evidence of sensitivity to touch and response to stimulation. This, however, is not a sign of consciousness but a non-conscious physical response. It had generally been held that foetal sential awareness only develops after 26 weeks and almost all abortions take place well before that stage. Recent evidence of hormonal responses, however, points to foetuses reacting as if they were feeling pain as early as week 17 and some argue that it may be even earlier still. Although this would be later than most abortions, in the US usually over 40,000 abortions still take place each year after 17 weeks.

Rejecting abortion after this stage is an understandable emotional response – nobody should like inflicting pain – but its moral standing as a ground for the protection of the embryo's life is less clear. It would, after all, be possible to use anaesthesia before aborting (as in cases of late abortion), in which case there would be no pain. If pain were the only concern, abortion could then proceed with no moral difficulty. Furthermore, if experience of pain were the sole criterion then this would presumably also apply to the status of **animals** and animal experimentation.

Brain development

A stronger case can be made that the embryo becomes worthy of full respect when the development of its brain means it becomes much more clearly like us. Given that we now register death in terms of brain death (see **euthanasia**), perhaps we can recognize life that must be protected using similar criteria based on brain function.

However, exactly where the crucial line would be placed depends on how the word 'brain' is defined. The arrival of the primitive streak at 14 days is the first time that nervous tissue starts to develop, and prior to that there can be no nervous activity so no chance of even the most primitive brain activity. From as early as 22 days the embryo's neural tube has formed as the beginning of the brain and this quickly divides into the three parts that will develop into different parts of the brain. This, however, functions nothing like the human brain in the sense in which we mean it when we use it as a way of distinguishing humans from animals. As a result, it is hard to place any great significance on this early development. It takes several more weeks (probably about week 10) before there is electrical activity in the brain and even then there is no sign of this activity being organized.

Organized brain activity that could be registered on an EEG probably does not occur until much later, around week 25. Some have argued that this is the point at which the foetus eventually becomes like us in a morally significant manner, as it has conscious experiences and its life therefore must be protected. It not only has a human future like ours (which is true from conception), but the development of its brain means the foetus – like the newborn and the infant – now has the capability to desire, and this may include the desire not to be killed.

Viability

The biggest difficulty for those who support abortion but reject infanticide is that there are clearly situations in which the embryo, though still in the womb, would be able to survive outside the womb. There appears to be a moral difficulty in arguing that it is permissible to kill an embryo at a certain stage if it is in the womb but that killing it at exactly the same stage is murder if it has been born. In almost all cases where we are faced with the choice of either inducing labour and giving the embryo a chance of life outside the womb or performing an abortion the latter decision would be very difficult to justify.

Babies have now survived when born as early as 22 weeks. After 24 weeks the chance of survival in developed countries can be as high as 60 per cent, and this rises to 95 per cent at 26 weeks. It is largely as a result of these facts that there has been much debate recently about lowering the legal limit for abortions in the UK from 24 weeks.

Giving the grounds: Why abort?

At whatever stage of pregnancy abortion is considered, all would agree that it represents at least the intentional ending of the development of a life that has the potential to become a human person like you and me. As we have seen, most people would hold that at some stage – perhaps at every stage – it represents something closer to the killing of a human person. On either count, some sort of justification would appear to be necessary in order to explain *why* abortion was right. The grounds can be grouped under three categories:

- grounds related to the context of conception;
- grounds related to the situation of the woman;
- grounds related to the embryo.

Conception

In most cases the rationale for abortion can be broadly classed as 'unwanted pregnancy'. The strongest case for this is clearly where the pregnancy is the result of rape. At no point has the woman in any sense consented to the process that is now biologically leading her to becoming the mother of a new human being. The biggest challenge to those who take the 'absolute prohibition' line is whether the fact that they believe life begins at conception means that they therefore believe abortion – even use of the morning-after pill – is wrong after rape. While some would hold this position and argue that two wrongs don't make a right, many would say that such situations must be understood and handled differently. The pregnancy is, in this case, an ongoing assault on the woman's body, a sort of extension of the rape itself. The woman is therefore not required to respond to it as she would to conception after consensual sexual intercourse.

This argument can be extended further to argue that if the woman had no intention of becoming pregnant when she engaged in sexual intercourse then she may have grounds for considering abortion. This would be even more persuasive in cases where precautionary contraceptive measures were taken but failed. Clearly this stance is not going to convince those who believe abortion even at the earliest stage is equivalent to killing a human person but, especially if combined with other grounds, it may be persuasive for those with other perspectives.

The pregnant woman

The strongest arguments for abortion will relate to the effect of the pregnancy on the woman. She is the one whose life, certainly for the next eight or nine months, possibly for many years, is most affected by the pregnancy. However, claiming that being 'pro-choice' gives adequate reason for the decision to abort is insufficient justification. Such an emphasis on choice gives no explanation, no reason as to why the choice is made. There can be no doubt that in the overwhelming majority of cases the decision to abort is a serious, difficult and often painful moral decision. However, there are also – at least theoretically – possible reasons for choosing an abortion that are frivolous, such as a concern about being pregnant during the summer when one likes to wear a bikini. It is, therefore, not unreasonable to expect some rationale to be offered for a decision to abort, whatever one's views on the status of the embryo. More substantive reasons generally relate to the domestic or medical situation of the mother.

Domestically, it may be that the relationship within which the child was conceived has ended or that the family appears unable to cope financially or emotionally with an additional member. Medically, the mother's physical or mental health may be such that either the pregnancy itself or the birth of the child is considered to be too great a burden. Reasons such as these represent the legal grounds given for almost all abortions in the UK. Here the decision made will be based on consideration of the severity of the problem and the suffering it causes, and the judgment made as to the status of the embryo. The higher someone's view of the status of the embryo and of the responsibility of a woman to receive the new life nurtured in pregnancy as a good gift, the stronger the negative effects of continuing with the pregnancy will have to be.

The classic dilemma is clearly where the mother's health or very life is seriously threatened by the pregnancy. In extreme cases a choice may need to be made between the life of the mother and the life of the embryo. Here a distinction is sometimes drawn between 'direct' and 'indirect' abortion. Direct abortion is the willed and intended ending of life in the womb. Indirect abortion is when some other medical treatment is required for the woman's health that indirectly ends the developing life (such as a hysterectomy or radiotherapy as treatments for cancer of the womb which results in the death of an embryo *in utero*). Even conservative Roman Catholic teaching allows for indirect abortions in certain situations.

An even more difficult situation is when the developing pregnancy itself presents the risk and so needs to be directly ended in order to preserve the mother's well-being. Here even many who would strongly oppose most cases of direct abortion recognize that, as with rape, the situation is significantly different. The growing embryo – however innocently – represents a material attack upon the mother who may need to defend herself in such a way that the embryo is destroyed. Furthermore, as someone who has moral responsibilities and bonds of affection established already (for example, in relation to existing family), the mother's life would generally be considered to have a stronger claim to preservation than that of the unborn embryo.

Some, however, would take a different view. In May 2004, Pope John Paul II declared Gianna Beretta Molla a saint of the Roman Catholic Church. A physician and surgeon and mother of three, during her fourth pregnancy she was diagnosed with an ovarian cyst. Nevertheless, she refused treatment of the cyst as it would have led to the death of the child she was carrying. As a result, she died in 1962 aged 39, one week after giving birth to the child. Here is a real example of a 'good Samaritan' pregnancy, although some critics argue that Molla neglected her maternal duties to her existing children by refusing treatment. Even among those who respect such a decision, many would argue that such self-sacrifice is not *required*, and so while it may be honoured it must not be expected of all women in such situations.

The embryo

The third group of grounds for justifying abortion relate to the embryo being aborted. Here the focus is not on the health or well-being of the woman but on the embryo itself. The judgment is made that the embryo's future life is likely to be so poor that it is better for it not to come to term and be born. This decision to deprive a developing human life of reaching its goal clearly raises a number of ethical issues.

First, there is the question of what any such selection says about our attitudes to those living people who share the physical condition that justifies aborting the embryo. Some of the most interesting and passionate critics of abortion are those who are themselves disabled in some way and see embryos that would become people like them being considered as legitimate objects of abortion. Decisions to abort on the grounds of handicap raise questions about the eugenic mentality this represents. It is reasonable to ask whether any society can take this attitude to the existence of embryos suffering from such impairments while continuing fully to respect and treat as equals those children and adults who share their condition. If it is judged that the life of an embryo in the womb with such a condition would not be worth living then it may prove difficult never to translate such a judgment into a discriminatory attitude to those who are alive.

Some have even argued that in at least some cases parents have a responsibility or even a duty to abort, and that failure to do so should be seen as immoral and even worthy of being sued for 'wrongful life'.

Second, there is the question of what forms of handicap justify abortion and to what stage in the pregnancy. Under UK law, abortions can be carried out with no time limit if 'there is a substantial risk that if the child were born it would suffer from such physical or mental abnormalities as to be seriously handicapped'. In order to discourage late abortions, it is now standard practice to offer pregnant women tests early in pregnancy for conditions such as Down's Syndrome even though the only medical 'remedy' should the test prove positive is abortion. The problems raised by the lack of a legal definition of 'serious handicap' were highlighted in 2003 when the Revd Joanna Jepson hit the headlines. She challenged in the courts – as yet still unsuccessfully – the legality of a late abortion on a 28-week embryo that had been justified on the grounds that the embryo had a cleft palate. Although it is very unusual for such an extremely late abortion to be performed for such a minor abnormality (Jepson herself had suffered from facial disfigurement and has a brother with Down's Syndrome), it demonstrates the breadth of moral assessments that can be made within the law.

Third, there is the challenge of whether those strongly opposed to abortion will ever grant that it may be legitimate in cases of very serious deformity of the foetus. It may be that the life to be lived would be so inherently terrible – almost a form of torture – that it is judged it should not be inflicted on anyone, or it may be that the embryo is doomed to die either at or very soon after birth. Thankfully, such conditions as anencephaly (where there is only a brain stem) or Edward's Syndrome (which involves a range of serious symptoms) are relatively rare. They do, however, raise the question as to whether abortion in these cases – even if not in situations of milder conditions – might be considered legitimate.

Fourth, there is the case of Mandy Allwood which hit the headlines in 1996. She found she was carrying eight embryos and was offered selective abortion. This would have ended the lives of six of the embryos in the womb with the intention that two of them would then have been able to develop to term. In fact, Allwood chose (with the support of anti-abortion groups) to reject the offer and shortly afterward she miscarried all eight. Although this is an extreme case, selective reduction is offered in other cases of multiple pregnancy.

Making the decision: Who decides?

The final key ethical question is how the decision whether or not to abort a particular pregnancy is made. It is clear that the embryo is unable to be involved in this process. Some argue that its powerlessness and voicelessness requires others to speak on its behalf, and obliges the law to defend its life. However, it is also clear that the person most directly affected by the pregnancy and by any abortion is the woman whose very body is the object of any law on abortion. She is, nevertheless, not the only other 'interested party'. Even before it is born, the embryo is placed within a wider network of relationships. Most obviously there is a biological father who may have strong views concerning whether to terminate the pregnancy. The most common situation is probably the man pressuring the woman to have an abortion but the woman refusing. There are, however, cases where the man has complained that his partner securing an abortion is depriving him of his right to become a father. In legal cases in both the UK and the US, partners who were biological fathers of the developing child have failed to prevent a woman proceeding with an abortion.

Should there be no legal limits placed on the woman making the decision? Some argue for a law that enshrines a woman's absolute 'right to choose' even until the very latest stages of pregnancy. Most, however, believe that some sort of regulation by the law is necessary. Here clearly all the issues discussed above need to be considered. It would be wrong to think that the law can simply ignore the moral issues. However, there must be recognition that when the discussion is about legalities rather than morality the debate becomes more complicated. Two issues in particular may justify someone making a distinction between what they believe is morally right (and thus what they would do and would justify in their own ethical decision-making and what they would advise others to do) and what they believe the law should state on abortion.

First, the law has coercive force and limits the freedom of moral choices available to women, not least by threatening them with some form of punishment if they violate the law. For this reason most accept that there may be some actions that can be considered 'immoral' but that these need not therefore be made illegal. Second, the law has to be enforceable and so must have reasonable support in society. The law quickly falls into disrepute if it seeks to be stricter than the broad consensus among those it seeks to regulate. Making abortions illegal also runs the risk that they will continue to happen but in contexts that are less safe for women, and it was the rise in such 'back-street' abortions that first led to calls for a change in the law in the 1960s.

Conclusion

Abortion is one of the most emotive and politically charged of all the ethical issues discussed in this book, especially in the US. It is an action that is remarkably common in Western society but which some see (in many if not all cases) as a form of legalized murder.

Those opposed to abortion can and do raise powerful arguments in support of their stance, but if a stance is taken against abortion then perhaps what is even more important than arguments are actions. In 1997 the then Roman Catholic archbishop of Glasgow, Thomas Winning, created quite a furore by declaring the commitment of his diocese to supporting women who might be considering abortion. He gave an open invitation to any woman, family or couple faced with an unwanted pregnancy to seek assistance: 'Whatever worries or cares you may have… we will help you. If you need pregnancy testing or counselling… we will help you. If you want help to cope with raising the baby on your own… we will help you. If you want to discuss adoption of your unborn child… we will help you. If you need financial assistance, or help with equipment for your baby and feel financial pressures will force you to have an abortion… we will help you. If you cannot face your family, or if pressure in your local area is making you consider abortion, come to us, we will help find you somewhere to have your baby surrounded by support and encouragement. We will help you.'

Although some accused him of putting pressure on women to follow his own views on the subject by offering support, counselling and adoption, he was clearly seeking to provide alternatives for the many women who may not want an abortion but feel that termination is their only option. Pope John Paul II claimed the current high frequency of abortion in Western societies is a symptom of what he called a 'culture of death'. For those who share this view, perhaps the strongest ethical response is not a political campaign to change the law or the moralistic condemnation of those who have abortions, but the creation of a positive counterculture that welcomes and supports those struggling with the gift of a new human life in the midst of suffering.

5. Genetics

'You see, (s)he's not genetically modified.' My wife and I sometimes use this phrase when we are struck by how similar one of our children is to one of us. It's a phrase that my own parents would not have used – even though my father is a biochemist. And for his parents it would have been literally unthinkable. This is because the area of genetics is the field of science that has perhaps seen the most rapid and the most significant advances in the last half-century and which promises even more amazing discoveries and developments in the decades ahead. Before beginning to sketch some of the current and possible future ethical challenges that arise from these developments, it is necessary to get a basic grasp of the science involved.

Unravelling the genome

The birth of modern genetics is usually dated to 1953, when the Cambridge-based scientists James Watson and Francis Crick discovered the 'double helix' structure of 'deoxyribonucleic acid' (thankfully known as 'DNA' for short). This has been called the most important discovery in human history and the scientific insight that has most changed human self-understanding. Fifty years later, after thirteen years of research, the Human Genome Sequencing Consortium announced in April 2003 that it had succeeded in determining the sequence of 99 per cent of the human genome and that it had done so with 99.99 per cent accuracy. But what exactly is going on here? The science is obviously complex (and it's not essential to understand it all to grasp the ethical issues), but it's worth trying to know the basics.

In the human body there are roughly 100 million million (or 100,000,000,000,000!) cells which have various functions (for example, nerve cells, skin cells). Inside the nucleus of each miniscule cell (about 0.01 mm in diameter) there are 46 'chromosomes' coiled up. These are arranged in 23 pairs, and each pair includes one chromosome from each parent. It is these 46 chromosomes that collectively make up the human 'genome' – the complete genetic instructions for human constitution and physiology.

Packaged in each of these chromosomes is one long molecule of double helical DNA. Each of these molecules contains two strands that are composed of millions of units joined together. These units (called 'nucleotides') consist of a sugar ('deoxyribose' – hence 'deoxyribonucleic acid'), a phosphate group and one of four 'bases', labelled A, G, T and C (from the first letter of their chemical names). The nucleotide units are joined together by bonds between the sugar of one unit and the phosphate group of the next. Any one of the four bases (A, G, T and C) can be attached to each sugar on this repeating sugar–phosphate backbone. As a result, there are many possible ways in which the bases can be arranged. The order in which they appear is known as the 'base sequence' or 'nucleotide sequence'. Two joined units could be positioned in 16 ways; three units in 64 ways; and the number of possible sequences in a 100-unit DNA strand is greater than 1 followed by 60 noughts!

The genetic information contained in the DNA can be copied when cells divide because the bases on one strand of the DNA double helix pair up with specific bases on the second strand (A with T and C with G). They therefore form 'base pairs'. These can be visualized as the rungs of a twisted spiral ladder that is the DNA within the chromosomes. There are currently estimated to be about 3 billion of these base pairs in the human genome, although most of these sequences in the genome appear to have no obvious or significant function.

The most important sequences are the 'genes' and the control sequences that are used to turn those genes on or off. Recent research suggests that there are probably about 25,000 working genes in the human genome. These genes contain the information that helps cells to produce 'proteins' which then become the building blocks of each cell or enable it to perform its various functions. Proteins are made up of chains of 'amino acids' and up to twenty different amino acids can be used to produce any particular protein. What each protein does in the cell depends on its sequence of amino acids. This sequence is itself determined by the information supplied in the base sequence of the gene. Thus there is a direct link between the base sequence and the structure and function of the cell.

Although every human cell has all 25,000 genes, most of them are 'turned off' so that their information is not available to make proteins. When cells read the information of different genes, they make different proteins and therefore become different types of cells. One exception to this is embryonic 'stem cells'. These are present very early in development, before the cells turn individual genes 'on' or 'off' and differentiate into different cell types. As we shall see, these stem cells are an important area of ethical debate.

Genes, then, are comprised of DNA and they make a sort of 'instruction manual' for the working of our bodies. Different forms of the same gene (for example, the different forms of the gene for eye colour which determine whether your eyes are blue, brown or green) are known as 'alleles'.

Different genes perform different functions and if something goes wrong within the DNA – what is called 'genetic mutation' – then the part of the body 'run' by that gene will not work properly. So, for example, the haemoglobin genes produce the protein haemoglobin that captures and carries oxygen around our bodies in red blood cells. If something goes wrong with this gene then a disease such as sickle cell anaemia may result.

There is still much more to discover about our genes but the increasing knowledge about our human genetic make-up already raises a whole range of ethical questions. At the heart of these are what we are to do with such new knowledge and whether our new insights will prove to be a source of great good and promise or a danger and a threat to human well-being and development.

Making people better: gene therapy

The great hope many have in increased genetic technology is that it will enable us to tackle health problems that have so far escaped human remedy. We are still faced with many crippling diseases for which standard medicine has been unable to find a cure. There is the possibility that, with advances in knowledge of the human genome and developments in genetic engineering, we may discover the underlying genetic malfunctions and so be able to offer a remedy in the form of gene therapy.

Gene therapy is genetic intervention (through some form of manipulation, compensation or eradication) used in response to an inherited genetic defect in order to bring healing to a patient.

Many diseases are caused by such faulty genes being passed on from parent to child. In addition to sickle cell anaemia noted above there are hopes that cystic fibrosis, muscular dystrophy and perhaps a much wider range of conditions could be treated by gene therapy. The usual form of intervention would be to insert a normal working gene somewhere into the patient's genome in order that the patient then has the DNA necessary to perform the task that the body is currently failing to fulfil properly. Alternative forms of therapy would be to 'swap' the abnormal allele for a normal one, or to 'repair' the faulty allele by seeking to reverse the mutations that led it to stop performing its task effectively and so render the patient ill.

The simple fact is that all of these forms of therapy still remain in a development stage. The difficulties both of knowing what DNA is needed to remedy any particular disease and delivering that DNA safely into the patient (usually by means of a virus genetically altered to include human DNA) without causing further complications remain major challenges. This creates major dilemmas for people like 30-year-old Anthony Harold who suffers from Chronic Granulomatous Disorder (CGD), a disease caused by a faulty bone marrow gene. CGD means he cannot fight off infections properly and scarring to his lungs makes breathing difficult. He has been given only two years to live, but it is possible that using gene therapy may provide him with the genetic material he needs. However, as the therapy is still at a very early stage, the treatment has major risks, including that of contracting cancer.

The ethical challenges attached to gene therapy are, at one level, no different from those connected with any other form of medical treatment, especially at the early stages of development. In particular, decisions need to be made about the risks as well as the potential benefits of new procedures. There are, however, two new sets of moral issues that arise when it becomes possible to engage in human genetic engineering.

The first of these is based on the distinction between 'somatic cells' and 'germ cells' within the human body. Germ cells are those cells involved in the production of sperm or eggs and so with the passing of genetic material from one generation to the other. In contrast, somatic cells are cells that simply constitute and control the body of the individual.

If gene therapy were carried out only on somatic cells then it would simply mark a major advance in our ability to treat a patient with a particular disease. The patient's children, however, will not be able to receive the properly functioning gene. They may (depending on their precise genetic constitution) receive the defective one and so risk falling prey to the same illness as their parent. Gene therapy on stem cells, however, raises the possibility of altering the faulty cells not just of the suffering patient but also of all their descendants, thus eliminating the genetic flaw from that family's overall genetic make-up.

At one level there would appear to be no major moral objection to germ cell therapy. After all, it simply seeks to prevent the future occurrence of diseases we currently seek to cure when they present in one individual. Indeed, some would argue that refusing to develop germ cell gene therapy and restricting our genetic research and development to somatic cell therapy is immoral. This is because such a restriction fails to grasp the possibility of eliminating suffering on a wide scale and leaves people able to benefit only themselves and not their offspring. Indeed, it is increasingly likely that when germ cell therapy is not available and there is a risk of serious genetic illness, people will opt for pre-implantation genetic diagnosis to screen embryos (see **IVF**) or **abortion** as a means of preventing the birth of a seriously handicapped child.

There are, however, concerns raised by the possibility of germ cell therapy. It represents a novelty which some have claimed is a therapy which is developed and offered not to benefit an existing ailing patient but to benefit the human race as a whole. Particularly when there are uncertainties about the possible side effects of such genetic manipulation, serious questions can be raised as to whether we are right to make decisions that so decisively affect future generations, even if we do so out of a desire for their good and their well-being. Can we really be so sure that we know what is best for them? Some have also expressed concern about what such forms of therapy implicitly say to those who continue to be born with and suffer from these genetic diseases. Is it possible both to seek to eliminate particular diseases from future generations by means of germ cell therapy and also to treat those who suffer from them as equal and valued members of society?

As a result of such concerns the Council of Europe's 1997 Convention on Human Rights and Biomedicine includes the statement that 'An intervention seeking to modify the human genome may only be undertaken for preventive, diagnostic or therapeutic purposes and only if its aim is not to introduce any modification in the genome of any descendants' (Article 13). This effectively prohibits the application of germ cell therapy at present.

The opening limitation stated in Article 13 – that genetic intervention must be for 'preventive, diagnostic or therapeutic purposes' – raises the second and even more difficult ethical challenge presented by gene therapy.

Making better people?

There are certain conditions that everyone will readily grant are diseases that medicine should seek to heal. However, the increase in knowledge about our genetic make-up may well enable us to see and then to alter how our genes shape us in other ways. It may therefore be possible to use gene 'therapy' for what many would consider to be non-therapeutic ends such as personal enhancement. The difficult questions are whether and how one can distinguish between therapeutic and non-therapeutic or enhancing procedures and whether enhancements are inherently immoral and therefore to be rejected. In some cases the distinction appears obvious: genetic intervention to counter cystic fibrosis is therapeutic; to change eye colour is not. But what about increasing a person's height? Which category does that fall in? Is it 'therapeutic' if the patient suffers from dwarfism but not if they are simply 'naturally small'?

And what, anyway, is wrong with enhancement? Most of the time we are seeking to improve ourselves and encouraging our children to do the same. We want to become better than we are at present, whether that is in relation to sport or career or some other area of our lives. Is there anything inherently immoral about securing such betterment at least in part by the use of genetic knowledge and engineering?

As we face the possibility that some of these choices may become real in the near future, one of the underlying concerns is that we will see (and indeed are already beginning to see) the revival of 'eugenics'. The modern eugenics movement originated with the English scientist Francis Galton (1822–1911) and gained prominence in the early twentieth century, climaxing horrifically in the eugenic policy of the Nazis. Eugenics sought to better the human race both by 'positive' means (such as encouraging those of 'higher quality' to reproduce) and by 'negative' means, which sought to reduce or even eliminate those considered to be 'weak' or of 'lower stock'. Already it could be argued that **abortion** and some forms of genetic screening of embryos (see the discussion of designer babies in the chapter on **IVF**) amount to a form of eugenics. Some have expressed fears that the acceptance of **euthanasia** may also have this effect. The danger becomes even more serious in the light of the possibilities that could be opened up by genetic engineering.

At present of course this is hypothetical, but it is always best – though not always possible or achievable – for the ethical issues to be raised and considered before a new technological development is realized rather than once it has been established and is available for use. In our current culture it would appear that, while there is no risk of the recurrence of the Nazi-style forced eugenics, a new form of genetic selection and preferment might begin to develop. In liberal and consumerist societies the pressure will be to allow great space for individual freedom and choice over what 'goods' to seek by means of genetic intervention. Attempts to prohibit genetic treatments that are viewed as 'enhancement' will be difficult to defend. This is especially so when the distinction between 'therapeutic' and 'non-therapeutic' measures is so difficult to define and there is a general acceptance that people can seek to 'enhance' themselves and seek the best for their children by other non-genetic means. Why should genetic manipulation be an illegitimate means to the same end? One of the marks of contemporary postmodern society is the construction – and often continuous re-construction – of our personal identity. In a society where cosmetic surgery is increasingly popular it is not unreasonable to assume that genetic surgery, once it becomes available, will also find a ready market in people's desire to meet their felt needs and to overcome what they experience as unacceptable limits to their quest for full humanity.

The difficulty is that, while apparently privileging personal autonomy, such a 'free market' approach to these possible developments in genetic medicine fails to consider two important factors. Firstly, recourse to such treatments will always be subject to economic constraints. This means there will be a great disparity between what is available to the rich and to the poor. Those who are already 'better off' are most likely to seek and secure 'enhancement' and thus social and other inequalities are likely to increase. Secondly, the cumulative effect of individual choices – though obviously not as controlling and destructive as state policies such as those of Nazi Germany – will shape a culture's vision of what it means to be a 'good person'. Those who are furthest from this ideal, physically, mentally and in other ways, will risk feeling marginalized and being treated as less than equal.

Genetic knowledge

At present our skills in genetic engineering make almost all these questions about possible forms of engineering and therapy rather hypothetical. The more pressing challenges relate to the possibility – especially with the advances brought by the Human Genome Project – that we may know quite a lot about our genetic make-up but be able to do very little about it.

For example, it may be that a range of character traits prove to have at least some genetic component. In addition to claims about a 'gay gene' linking sexual orientation to a part of one human chromosome, recent studies have argued that a person's level of aggression is also related to their DNA. There have already been cases in which those accused of particular crimes have sought to bring in evidence of a genetic predisposition to violence as part of their defence. This raises the deeper philosophical question of the extent to which genetic composition is either determinative of, or at least a valid mitigating circumstance for, a person's conduct. Both law and ethics (and our various understandings of **punishment**) depend on the acceptance that we all have a certain level of individual personal responsibility for our actions, and as yet the evidence in favour of any form of genetic determinism is very weak. Nevertheless, as our knowledge of genetic causes of (or at least predisposition to) certain character traits or patterns of behaviour improves, challenges that this knowledge amounts to a form of 'diminished responsibility' are likely to increase.

Much more concrete and already well established are genetic tests for certain diseases and for a person's propensity to develop certain diseases. Currently such tests are most widely used in situations where there is a known genetically-based ailment in a family that may also prove to be present but is as yet latent in other family members. Here, particularly if there are patterns of behaviour that can increase or reduce the risk of the disease developing, genetic knowledge may clearly be of benefit. However, in many cases there may be little that someone can do once they learn they have the allele that causes the problem and it may then be unclear what value there is in gaining such knowledge.

Such testing of family members arises, of course, once it becomes clear that there is a genetic disorder present in a close relative. That requires disclosure on the part of the patient with the disease. Here ethical tensions may arise between respect for patient confidentiality and the well-being of other family members. Experts in the field have revealed quite different assessments of the relative importance of these two goods. A House of Commons Science and Technology Committee concluded that 'if counselling cannot persuade someone to consent to sharing information with their relatives the individual's decision to withhold information should be paramount', but the Nuffield Council on Bioethics allowed that 'in exceptional circumstances, health professionals might be justified in disclosing genetic information to other family members, despite an individual's desire for confidentiality'.

If providing information to family members can create some ethical dilemmas, the issues become even more complex in relation to other groups, notably employers and insurers. It is generally accepted that both of these groups may legitimately seek medical reports before employing or agreeing to insure a person. If this is so, then as genetic information becomes more easily retrievable and interpretable it must be asked whether this is also knowledge that others may request and make a condition for provision of employment or medical insurance.

The fear here is clearly that individuals may be unjustly discriminated against on the basis of genetic information. People may be refused a job or offered insurance at higher premiums (if at all) if they refuse to provide what is requested or if what is requested gives cause for concern that they are a high risk. The Council of Europe's Convention asserts that 'any form of discrimination against a person on grounds of his or her genetic heritage is prohibited', but there may be situations in which 'discrimination' is justifiable. If, for example, someone's genetic make-up means they are much more likely to contract illnesses that are occupational hazards in a certain line of work then it may be important that information is available to both employee and employer (especially if that risk has implications for other members of the workforce).

Each of these aspects of genetic knowledge relate to the particular details of an individual's DNA and its implications for their present and future health and well-being. A final ethical issue that must be noted under this heading is that of knowledge of particular genes and their function. Given the potential financial gains if gene therapies were to become successful and widely available, there is inevitably concern about who benefits from knowledge gained in genetic research. As a result it is now commonplace for genes – both human and animal – to be patented to give the 'inventor' certain property rights and to prevent others from using the gene. This 'patenting of life' has inevitably raised moral objections. These relate both to what is being done (is it really legitimate to patent the discovery of a gene which, after all, is part of nature, as if it were a human invention?) and to its consequences, as there are fears that the effect of widespread patenting will be to inhibit developments in gene therapy.

Cloning

Nearly a decade ago, on 5 July 1996, a sheep named Dolly hit the headlines. Her claim to fame was that she was the world's first cloned mammal. There had been clones before – the lowly tadpole was cloned as far back as 1952 – and more mammal clones have been created since – pigs in 2000 and a horse in 2003. But Dolly will remain the icon of cloning.

The process used was 'somatic cell nuclear transfer' (SCNT).

This involves taking genetic material from the nucleus of a donor adult cell and transferring it to an egg cell whose genetic material has been removed. This is then treated in order to stimulate cell division and, if it all works, following implantation, a creature is born with the same DNA or genetic makeup (hence a 'clone') as that of the donor. The use of cloning and other forms of genetic manipulation in **animals** raises a number of ethical issues (see also the discussion of genetically modified crops in the chapter on the **environment**), but it is inevitably human cloning that causes most concern and interest.

An important ethical distinction again needs to be drawn within the general category of cloning. This is between 'reproductive cloning' – in other words, creating a new animal with the same DNA as the original donor (as with Dolly) – and 'therapeutic cloning'. In therapeutic cloning there is no intention to reproduce, but rather to create stem cells that may prove of value in treating forms of disease and disability.

Long before Dolly, human reproductive cloning was the stuff of science fiction and rather ridiculous movie plots (such as the 1978 film *The Boys from Brazil*). It remains, as far we know, in the realm of fiction despite occasional claims to the contrary – including those of a rather bizarre religious sect called the Raëlians in 2002. The procedure of implanting a cloned human embryo in a womb is outlawed in most countries.

For some, the fundamental moral objection to any such attempt is a practical one related to the risks involved. Dolly was only conceived after nearly 300 attempts and her relatively early death after developing arthritis has raised concerns about the impact of being cloned on the health and life expectancy of any human clone. For many, however, the objection goes beyond the pragmatics of cost–benefit analysis to the belief that human reproductive cloning, even if not performed out of some ego-maniacal desire for a clone of oneself, would extend the procedures of **artificial reproductive technologies** too far. It purposefully creates a human person with the same DNA as a living person and the social and psychological effects of raising a child who is effectively the genetic twin of one of the parents are unlikely to be conducive to the child's good.

Much more contentious – and now a reality – is the practice of therapeutic cloning which was first made legal in the UK in 2001. In both the UK and South Korea, human embryos have recently been cloned as part of the quest for embryonic stem cells. These are sought because stem cells, especially when they are at an early stage of embryonic development, are pluripotent (in other words, they have the potential to turn into many types of cell). It is therefore hoped that, in addition to enabling us to understand more about cell development (with possible consequent benefits for the treatment of developmental disorders), research on embryonic stem cells may enable them to be cultured and manipulated in order to create healthy tissue for various parts of the body. The use of cloned embryos is important because it allows the creation of cells that would be a perfect match for the adult donor and so avoids the risk of rejection by the body.

Although this procedure has caused considerable moral controversy, this has not revolved around issues of genetic engineering. Few if any people would, it appears, object to experimenting with adult stem cells (which are found in certain mature, adult tissues and have similar properties to embryonic stem cells, though there are also some important differences). Indeed, some claim that these cells should be the focus of research and development and that their availability makes the use of embryonic stem cells strictly unnecessary. The concerns raised relate more to the issue of the status of the **embryo** and the fact that human clones are being purposefully created with no intention except that they be 'harvested' for stem cells and, in the process, destroyed. Some have also expressed concern that once cloned embryos are being widely produced as part of therapeutic cloning processes, it is only a matter of time before someone takes the next step and seeks to implant one in a womb and so attempt reproductive cloning.

Conclusion

The significance of genes in human identity, the relative newness of genetic technology, and the often exaggerated claims that are sometimes made about its potential power have led to major ethical concerns. It is often claimed that genetic intervention is 'playing God' and is therefore fundamentally wrong. There are clearly real ethical issues raised by both current and possible future developments but the use of such religious language and blanket condemnation is generally unhelpful.

After all, from a Christian viewpoint humans are in one sense meant to 'play God'. They are made in God's image, they have been given considerable powers, and they are meant to rule God's world. Furthermore, in all sorts of ways – in politics and long-established practices in medicine – we already act in ways that could be classified as 'playing God' and so genetic intervention is not unique. For Christians therefore, the problem is not so much that humans 'play God'. It is rather that they often do so without recognizing any God-given limits and without following the loving, self-giving and sacrificial pattern of God's rule and use of power that is seen in Jesus.

In relation to genetics, and many other areas, the real danger is an underlying spirit that seeks to use our knowledge and powers simply to satisfy our own desires and to strengthen the rich and powerful at the expense of the poor and weak. When we 'play God' in that way, recognizing no authority greater than ourselves and desiring greater control and power for our own ends, then we are not 'playing God' as we should. In fact, we run the risk of repeating the error recounted in the story found in Genesis 11, in which the people of Babel attempted to show their independence from God by uniting in a grand technological project to make a name for themselves, which ended in confusion and failure. By seeking to make a name for ourselves we may find we end up instead causing greater confusion, division and conflict.

6. War

It is estimated that in the twentieth century over 120 million people died in wars, whether civil wars or international conflicts. The century also saw an increase in the proportion of civilian deaths. During the First World War, about 90 per cent of the 13 to 15 million people who were killed were soldiers and only 10 per cent were civilians. By the end of the century, however, it was estimated that the number of civilian casualties of war made up roughly 75 per cent of the total.

Such horrific figures of the mass destruction of human life clearly present us with a major ethical challenge as we enter the twenty-first century. Wars – unlike natural disasters such as earthquakes and tsunamis – are not outside human control and decision-making. Can we therefore continue to justify waging war? If we do, how do we limit and control its evil effects?

Very broadly speaking, there are two main traditions of moral thought both among Christians and in the wider ethical debate. On the one hand, pacifism rejects participation in war and violence. On the other hand, the tradition of 'just war' accepts that some wars may be morally justified but seeks to limit and control warfare by appealing to justice.

Pacifism

Among those who would be classed as pacifist there is a great variety of explanations for and defences of their absolute moral opposition to war. John Howard Yoder, one of the leading Christian pacifists of the twentieth century, identified no less than 29 'varieties of religious pacifism'. At least, despite their differences, they shouldn't start a war with each other! To over-simplify, it is possible to distinguish between two lines of argument among pacifists. Some are more based on practicalities and consequences – what might be called 'pragmatic pacifism'. Others express opposition to war on the basis of fundamental beliefs – what might be called 'principled pacifism'.

Pragmatic pacifism

Those who oppose war on pragmatic grounds argue both negatively from the horrific reality of war and positively from the benefits of non-violence.

In relation to violence, it is argued that war, as it is a destructive force, is incapable of producing a better situation. On the contrary, there is almost a sociological 'law of violence', namely that violence begets more violence. As recent conflicts in Northern Ireland and the former Yugoslavia vividly demonstrate, contemporary wars are regularly fuelled by a history – sometimes a very old history – of past violence that has not been forgiven and wars that have not been forgotten.

On an even more serious note, much of contemporary culture seeks to deny this basic fact by teaching us all from an early age the myth of redemptive violence. Stories, cartoons, TV programmes and movies give the message that violence is a valid way of putting things right in the world. This perhaps explains why violence and war also seem to have an almost addictive aspect to them such that once we start using violence we find it very difficult to stop. This is exaggerated even further by the fact that there are structures of economic and political power – what President Eisenhower back in 1961 famously called the 'military-industrial complex' – that reinforce this outlook and, through the arms trade and propaganda, encourage recourse to war. In order to combat such lies and to resist such powers pacifists argue that there must be no compromise but rather a total and absolute rejection of all war.

One of the common objections to pacifism is that it offers no practical alternative to war. It is therefore morally irresponsible and in practice advocates a pattern of withdrawal from the harsh realities of life in the world. In response, some pacifists will point instead to the positive effects of following the pacifist way. Rather than reading history as we are generally taught it in schools – in terms of wars and battles – non-violent movements and patterns of civil disobedience can be highlighted as means of effecting social change and resisting injustice. Examples from the twentieth century include not only Gandhi's passive resistance to British imperial rule in India but also the bringing to an end of both the Soviet bloc and apartheid in South Africa, without war and largely by non-violent means. Here the pragmatic pacifist argument is a positive one: not only does war not work, but other creative means of conflict resolution are effective. The problem is seen to be similar to that which G.K. Chesterton identified in relation to Christianity – pacifism has not been tried and found wanting; it has been found difficult and not tried. The challenge is, therefore, to resist the siren calls of those who urge recourse to war and to discover original, alternative, peace-loving and peace-making patterns of response to injustice and violence.

Principled pacifism

Principled pacifist arguments are not as dependent on consequences and effectiveness for their moral persuasive force. They might even accept the criticism that pacifism is less 'successful' as a strategy than war, at least in certain instances. Their concern is rather with pacifism as a matter of obedience to a command or witness to the truth. Among the many forms of pacifism there is an explicitly Christian rationale that must be considered.

It appears clear that, in the first few centuries, the Christian church was broadly pacifist. It was widely held, in the famous words of Tertullian (160–220), that 'the Lord, in subsequently disarming Peter, disarmed every soldier'. This argument is based on an incident recorded in all four gospels in which Jesus rebuked the disciple Peter for attacking a Roman soldier with a sword while attempting to prevent Jesus' arrest in the Garden of Gethsemane (see, for example, Matthew 26:52). Although from the fourth century onwards the pacifist position has tended to be a minority one among Christians, it has been represented in every age and remains an important feature of Christian responses to war. Its most significant recent advocates, writers such as Stanley Hauerwas and John Yoder, are particularly influenced by the Anabaptist or Mennonite tradition of the Radical Reformation. At its centre is its understanding of the teaching, the example, the person and the work of Jesus Christ.

The teaching of Jesus

The teaching of Jesus that pacifists mainly appeal to is his Sermon on the Mount, which is found in chapters five to seven of Matthew's Gospel. In particular Jesus calls his disciples in this passage to love their enemies (Matthew 5:43). They are not to resist an evildoer but are rather to 'turn the other cheek' (Matthew 5:39). This pattern of love in the face of enmity and violence is taken by pacifists to require Christians to reject all participation in war. It is reiterated in the rest of the New Testament. Apostles teach us not to repay evil with evil but to overcome evil with good as we bless those who persecute us (Romans 12:14–21). They call us to follow the pattern of Christ by not threatening others when we suffer but entrusting ourselves instead to God and his judgment (1 Peter 2:19–24).

The example of Jesus

This apostolic reference to the example of Jesus shows how Jesus put his own teaching into practice. At the heart of the Christian message is the cross of Jesus, which demonstrates that Jesus, though he suffered unjustly, did not resort to violence in response. Throughout his ministry he was at the heart of conflict and harassment but his approach was consistently one that rejected violent and coercive responses.

The person of Jesus

Even more fundamentally, Christians believe that in Jesus God reveals most fully who he really is and how he is at work in human history. Paul the apostle sums up the Christian good news as follows: while we were still God's enemies he showed his love to humanity by Christ dying for us. Christian pacifists argue that, as Jesus' death on the cross shows how God deals with his enemies, this is therefore how people made in God's image should deal with their enemies. The cross teaches that God is at work to set the world right. He has done so not through war and bloodshed but by non-violent, suffering love. That central message means that humans do not need to sort out and redeem the world themselves. God has already done that in

Christ and, Christian pacifists argue, this shows that we certainly cannot claim to be righting wrongs in a God-like manner if we do so by means of war.

Just war

In contrast to a pacifist rejection of all war, the mainstream Christian viewpoint has been willing to justify war under certain conditions. This 'just war tradition' has developed over the centuries and its central ideas are explored in the writings of such historical greats as Augustine (354–430), Aquinas (1225–74), Luther (1483–1546), Vitoria (1485–1546) and Grotius (1583–1645). Among its recent significant defenders are writers such as Paul Ramsey, James Turner Johnson and Oliver O'Donovan.

Sadly in much popular discussion – usually when a country is about to go to war – this pattern of thinking is reduced to a 'theory' or a scorecard of criteria. It becomes a sort of checklist of questions that people, by answering 'yes' or 'no', can use to decide whether or not a particular conflict is 'just'. In reality, the just war tradition is much more a whole way of thinking about war. As such, it seeks to limit recourse to war and moderate its excesses by relating it to the pursuit of justice by those with political authority. In that sense it reflects an outlook similar to that of Karl von Clausewitz, who famously commented that 'war is nothing but the continuation of politics with other means'. It insists, however, that politics is about the task of just judgment and righting wrong, not simply about the pursuit of power and the implementation of policies.

Many discussions of just war thinking tend to explain it by means of a list of criteria or tests. These are often divided into tests that must be applied before going to war (known technically as *jus ad bellum*) and criteria for use during the conflict itself (*jus in bello*). It is, perhaps, more helpful to explore such ethical thinking about war by asking four questions: Who? Why? When? And how?

Who?

The first limit the just war tradition places on waging war concerns *who* is able to do it. When Thomas Aquinas gave his non-pacifist answer to the question, 'Is it always sinful to wage war?', the first of the necessary conditions he gave for a war to be just was that it required 'the authority of the sovereign by whose command the war is to be waged'. This is now often expressed as the claim that war must be pursued by a 'legitimate authority'.

The reason for Aquinas's answer is crucial and marks one of the fundamental divisions between Christian pacifists and Christians who support 'just war'. This is the belief that there are certain actions that are acceptable when carried out by those with political authority (and those acting under their authority) that are *not* acceptable when carried out by private individuals. We accept this in relation to **punishment** within society. I have no authority to lock up another person but a judge and prison officers are legitimately able to treat someone who breaks the law in this way. The argument of the just war tradition is that this distinction extends by a similar line of reasoning to waging war. Bible passages such as Romans 13:1–7 in the New Testament are seen to support this distinction by granting a special role and authority from God to those with political authority.

In recent years this question has become particularly pressing in relation to the role of the United Nations. In 1990 at the time of the Iraqi invasion of Kuwait, the United Nations gave explicit support to an international military coalition. It did not, however, do so for either the 1999 intervention in Kosovo or for the second Gulf War waged principally by the US and the UK in 2003. Whatever the legal arguments concerning the authority for each of these wars, within the just war tradition's line of thinking they did not lack legitimate authority. This is because they were waged not by private armies but by governments. Of course those waging war would have had greater authority if they had received the support of the international community through the United Nations. Nevertheless, within just war thinking that is not strictly necessary for a nation to be justified in going to war.

The more fundamental challenge to this outlook is its perhaps excessive bias towards existing structures of authority. The implications of this became quite clear when Martin Luther urged the suppression of the Peasants' Revolt in his 'Against the Thievish and Murderous Hordes of Peasants' (1524). Many would argue that the tradition needs to adapt in order to facilitate 'just revolution' against existing corrupt political powers as well as 'just war'. This would mean finding some way in which, for example, Nelson Mandela and the ANC could have claimed to be a legitimate authority when they planned to oppose and overthrow the unjust apartheid system in South Africa.

Why?

The second prerequisite that Aquinas gives in his explanation of why war need not always be sinful was that 'a just cause is required, namely that those who are attacked should be attacked because they deserve it on account of some fault'. In its account of what constitutes a 'just cause', the just war tradition rejects two common attitudes used to defend wars.

- There is a tendency for war to be pursued and even justified by appeal to such phenomenon as national pride and self-interest, racial superiority or economic advantage. Undoubtedly many of the conflicts of the last century were driven by reasons much broader than, and much less defensible than, those proposed by Aquinas.
- Under the pressure of the horrors of war (especially the potential disaster of major war during the Cold War era using nuclear weapons) and pacifist lines of thought that led to a desire to eliminate war, it became common to treat 'self-defence' as the only justifiable grounds for war. In contrast, the just war tradition views war as justified only in response to a serious wrong being committed. This could include defending oneself from unjust attack but would extend beyond self-defence.

Another way of expressing this emphasis within just war thinking is to say that the tradition insists that those who wage war must have a *right intention*. Their goal in waging war must be to correct the wrong done and to restore a just and peaceful order to a situation that has been unjustly and violently disordered. In the paradoxical words of Augustine, 'we go to war in order that we may have peace'.

This response presents a challenge to Christian pacifist claims that pacifism is the only proper application of Jesus' teaching in the Sermon on the Mount. It argues not only that pacifism is in danger of forgetting the importance of justice but that war can also be a justifiable form of love for one's neighbour. When one neighbour attacks or wrongs another, neighbour-love demands some form of action in order to limit and reverse the wrong and to protect the weak and innocent party. That is why properly functioning political authority is an act of love. It may however be the case that such action will require the use of coercion and even of lethal force in certain circumstances.

In rejecting the limitation on the justification for going to war to 'self-defence', the just war tradition allows for the possible rightness of what are now called 'wars of intervention'. These are situations where a nation is not directly involved in some existing conflict or situation of injustice but steps in and initiates some form of interventionary military action. Writing this chapter on the tenth anniversary of the massacre of 8,000 Bosnian Muslims in Srebrenica is a reminder of the dangers of refusing to intervene when we are not personally threatened or attacked but there is ethnic cleansing taking place. The massacre of probably one hundred times that number of Rwandans in just one hundred days in 1994 stands as another testimony to the terrible truth of Edmund Burke's words that 'The only thing necessary for the triumph of evil is for good men to do nothing.'

There are, however, clearly dangers in justifying such interventionary wars. This is especially the case in a global situation in which one nation is the sole superpower. The risk is clearly that, rather than acting as a policeman in response to the demands of justice under the authority of the international community, it appears to intervene selectively and to do so not on the basis of justice but in order to preserve or advance its own interests.

When?

War, because it is such an extreme and destructive action and produces so many physical evils, is only to be waged as a necessity. It is not to be entered into lightly or rapidly but only after serious thought and after attempts have been made to secure justice by alternative peaceful and less destructive means. According to this view war is a 'last resort', just as capital **punishment**, if it is ever justifiable, is only acceptable in the most extreme situations when no other form of punishment can achieve the end that is required. This places a moral obligation on all those considering war to find alternative, preferably non-lethal, ways – such as diplomacy or a regime of sanctions – of responding to injustice.

War must also be used only when it has a 'reasonable prospect of success'. Here it is important that 'success' does not simply mean 'military success' but rather success in achieving the goal of a more just and peaceful social order. That, as the recent Iraq War and its aftermath have shown, is not always as easy to secure as the military defeat of the enemy army.

How?

The temptation is often to think that great care is needed when making decisions about going to war but that once the decision is made then the end justifies the means and 'anything goes' in the pursuit of victory. The just war tradition refuses to take such a 'realist' line. It insists that even amid the mayhem, trauma and horrors of fighting, moral questions must remain central and must determine decision-making. The two principles that should guide action are those of 'proportion' and 'discrimination'.

When deciding how to fight a war the actions that are permissible are limited both by what we are fighting against and what we are fighting to achieve. There is, in other words, a need both to look back and recall the wrong that led to war and to look forward and envision the good that the war seeks to secure. The principle of proportion says, in effect, 'Don't use a sledgehammer to crack a nut.' Just as it is acceptable to photograph and then fine speeding cars but it would be excessive to shoot their drivers, so we need to consider how serious the offence is which may lead to war. Some actions are not a proportionate or fitting response to the evil that is being done. For example, actions that were justified against Hitler would not have been justified against the Argentinians who invaded the Falkland Islands. Other actions are not fitted to serve the end that should be sought in war (for example, actions that destroy the social fabric necessary to establish a just and ordered peace after the conflict).

The tendency in war is often to go for 'overkill'. This is perhaps particularly the case if one has the advantage in terms of military power and if there is an excessive desire (as there often is in democratic regimes) to protect one's own troops from injury and death. This 'overkill' is sometimes tied to a dehumanization or even a demonization of the enemy that minimizes the significance of enemy casualties. The tradition of just war thinking insists, however, that our enemy is still a human neighbour whom we are called to love. It warns that all disproportionate use of force against an enemy is not justified but rather immoral. It calls therefore for the limitation of the level of force to the bare minimum necessary in order to right the wrong that caused the war and to secure the goal of a more justly ordered peace.

The language of 'discrimination' and the ethical issues it raises are captured in our sometimes rather disturbing jargon about 'legitimate targets' and 'collateral damage'. Discrimination demands that we don't treat the social body we wage war against as a single unit. Instead we must differentiate within it. Some of its members are directly and materially involved in the wrongdoing that has caused the war. Others are not involved in this way. Broadly speaking, this is the division we make between 'combatants' and 'non-combatants', although the parallel is not exact and the border between the two can appear blurred. The principle of discrimination insists that only 'combatants' should be directly and intentionally attacked. In other words, even in times of war there are a large number of people whom it is unacceptable to seek to kill or maim. Unlike the pacifist, however, the just war thinker permits lethal attacks on certain people as justifiable during war.

This does not, however, mean that whenever civilians die this is conclusive evidence that the attack was morally wrong. The principle of 'double effect' (also discussed under **euthanasia**) recognizes that there are situations in which a morally acceptable action (for example, bombing a military base) can have – and can be foreseen to have – effects that are neither intended nor desired (such as the 'collateral damage' of killing civilians in the vicinity of the base). The civilian deaths may be so great that they are disproportionate and so make the action unjustifiable. However, there will be cases in which the action is morally acceptable. This is because its intention and goal is right even if in its execution there are unintended and undesired side effects.

Discrimination does, however, rule out by definition any form of indiscriminate attack. Such attacks need to be condemned by any serious defender of just war thinking, whoever is responsible for them. They may take many forms: terrorist bombs on subways and buses, blanket aerial bombing of cities such as Dresden or Coventry or Tokyo, or the use of weapons of mass destruction such as the dropping of the nuclear bomb on Hiroshima. Here there is no sense in which civilian casualties are unfortunate and unintended. It makes neither military nor moral sense to unleash a nuclear weapon against a city and say, 'I have no intention to hurt innocent people.'

Conclusion

Within just war thinking the recourse to war can, perhaps, be helpfully compared to the recourse to surgery. It is a general rule that we do not invade the body of another human being. However, there are certain emergency situations in which – even without a patient's explicit consent – surgical interventions are considered justifiable and even right. They should, however, not normally be performed by just anyone but rather by someone with medical training and hence with authority. Surgery should also only be carried out when the patient is known to have a serious medical problem and the intention is to put that right, even if in the short-term it makes the patient's health worse. If that is not the case we are dealing with assault rather than surgery. If other and less drastic means can be found to solve the problem (such as a course of medication) then these should be attempted first. Surgery should also not be performed if there is little or no chance that it will resolve the problem. Finally, the surgery should be as limited as possible (for example, keyhole where possible); it should only focus on the cause of the problem (for example, the grumbling appendix) and should not involve direct interference in other parts of the body. If one translates this analogy from the treatment of specific sick organs within an individual's body to the response of war against specific agents of evil and injustice within a social body then the ethical lines of argument developed within the just war tradition are seen to be less unusual than we might perhaps initially believe.

However, even if one accepts there is some validity in such an analogy, it is vital to remember that, in addition to combating disease when it arises, we must also work for health. Simply waiting for sickness to arrive and then considering whether surgery is justifiable is totally insufficient and negligent.

Similarly, acting against injustice and disturbances of the peace when they arise is not enough, particularly when the means so often used – war – is itself the cause of some further injustice and certainly creates greater social disturbance. The pacifist challenge to develop non-violent means of conflict resolution and its commitment to establishing peace and working for reconciliation are therefore essential. Adherents to just war thinking, if they are serious about war being a last resort, have much to learn from these methods. Furthermore, from a Christian perspective, such pacifism can witness to the coming peaceable kingdom of God by resisting the ways of the world that are so frequently destructive of God's healthy, life-enhancing peace-with-justice which the Jewish scriptures call *shalom* and which the New Testament claims is embodied in Jesus of Nazareth.

7. Punishment

'If you do that one more time, I'll... ' From an early age we all become very aware of the phenomenon of punishment. It is perhaps one of the earliest moral issues to which we react, perhaps with the moral assessment that children so often make – 'That's not fair.' But what are we doing when we punish others and why do we do it? In particular what are we to make of two especially controversial forms of punishment: smacking children and capital punishment?

Understanding punishment

As is clear from the threatening words that opened this chapter and which are so often heard on a parent's lips, punishment only makes sense as a response to an earlier action. It is a reaction to wrongdoing. It is also an action that is properly carried out only by a person who has some recognized relationship of authority over the person who did the wrong. This may be a parent, a teacher, an employer or a judge.

The authority relationship is important because the act of punishment itself should be a negative experience for the one being punished ('If you do that one more time, I'll buy you a new computer game' is not a punishment!) If there is no recognized social structure of authority then there is a risk of 'punishment' being reduced simply to a tit-for-tat cycle of violence. After all, the similarities between what we do when we punish (fine, imprison, smack) and what it is that we are punishing (stealing, kidnapping, assault) are often very close. It is therefore important that punishment is set within the wider context of being a response by someone with authority to a prior wrongdoing.

What, then, can justify punishment? Can we really speak of it as something good? Traditionally, many ethicists have spoken of three 'theories of punishment': 'retributive' (punishment that is deserved and is a form of 'payback' for the wrong done); 'rehabilitative' (punishment that seeks to change the person who did wrong and enable them to become a better person); and 'deterrent' (punishment that discourages people from repeating the wrong). These theories clearly give some help in understanding punishment but they also create problems if they are treated in isolation or as grand theories. It is better to view punishment as seeking to achieve a number of different goals or goods.

Reinforcing the moral order
Punishment is based on belief in a moral order. It seeks to witness to this and to defend it by reacting negatively to violations of that order. In punishing someone we try to tell the truth about their actions by doing something that demonstrates to them and to others that they have done wrong. It is important in this case that the punishment is proportionate. In other words it should 'fit the crime': it should be neither too excessive nor too weak in its response to the seriousness of the offence. This relates to the 'retributive' theory of punishment. Though increasingly unpopular in our society – where it is often falsely viewed simply as a form of revenge – it is central to any understanding of punishment. After all, if someone has not done

anything wrong then they should not be punished even if punishing them might bring other benefits.

Vindicating the victim

Punishment recognizes that someone has been wronged by the person who is punished. It seeks both to vindicate the victim and to prevent them from seeking that vindication by their own means, which are likely to be disproportionate and driven by revenge. So parents usually intervene and punish their children rather than letting each child react when one of them wrongs another. Similarly, the criminal justice system is in part necessary to limit the danger of 'blood feuds' in which those who have been wronged, or their families, 'take the law into their own hands'.

Rehabilitating the offender

Punishment also seeks to do good to the person punished. It seeks to turn them away from their wrong choices and to encourage them to behave better in the future. Although this 'rehabilitative' approach is probably the most popular emphasis today, it is not without its difficulties. For example, the leniency of punishments can lead to protests that prisoners are being treated too well and that the wrong and the hurt they caused their victims has been forgotten. In previous centuries, however, it was the attempt to improve people that led to the development of penitentiaries and systems that would now be viewed as unduly harsh and oppressive.

Protecting society

Punishment also seeks the good of wider society. This may be through forms of punishment that restrict the liberty of the wrongdoer and so protect wider society from their actions. This could range from a simple 'go to your room' directed at a child for hitting a sibling through to imprisonment for crime. It may also take the form of 'deterrence': seeing what happens to those who do certain things will discourage others from repeating their errors. Again, however, the danger is that on its own this could lead to excessive punishment. Rather than deciding in the light of the offence, the severity of the punishment may be chosen on the basis of what will stop others from repeating it (*pour encourager les autres*).

Different people will emphasize different goals and so will ethically evaluate different forms and instances of punishment in different ways. With these various goals of punishment in mind we can look at two areas in which the form of punishment to be used is currently controversial and raises ethical questions. These are corporal punishment in the form of smacking children and capital punishment, or the execution of convicted criminals.

Corporal punishment

Corporal punishment involves inflicting physical pain on the body of the offender. In the UK the corporal punishment of criminals was abolished in 1948 and it has never been restored, despite occasional popular calls for using 'the birch' against young offenders. Corporal punishment remained legal in schools, however, for many years. My own schooling in Scotland in the 1970s and 1980s took place in the context of 'the belt' (or tawse), which could be used by teachers on disobedient pupils. It was only in 1986 that corporal punishment was legally abolished in state schools and it was not outlawed in private schools until 1998. In February 2005, however, some Christians involved in Christian schools took a court case to the House of Lords. They argued that this prohibition was an infringement of their religious freedom. They appealed to the principle, 'Spare the rod, spoil the child', derived from the Old Testament proverb, 'He who spares the rod hates his son, but he who loves him is careful to discipline him' (Proverbs 13:24). Parents, they claimed, could delegate to teachers their God-given right to apply physical punishment. They lost their case.

Despite this wider rejection of corporal punishment, in the UK certain physical punishment remains legal within the family and so parents are able to smack their children. Is this defensible, especially given its abolition in other spheres?

At the heart of the opposition to all corporal punishment of children is an argument based on the rights of the child. In 1989 the United Nations adopted the UNICEF Convention on the Rights of the Child. This included Article 19 which asserts that states should 'take all appropriate legislative, administrative, social and educational measures to protect the child from all forms of physical or mental violence, injury or abuse, neglect or negligent treatment, maltreatment or exploitation, including sexual abuse, while in the care of parent(s), legal guardian(s) or any other person who has the care of the child'.

British parents were for many years able to use 'reasonable chastisement' in relation to their children. In 2002, the United Nations Committee on the Rights of the Child criticized the 'reasonable chastisement' legal defence but, despite legal changes in 2004, attempts to make all smacking a crime failed. In recent years, however, a number of European countries, for example Germany in 2000, have made smacking illegal.

Although the rights-based argument against smacking is central to much campaigning, it suffers from the weakness that all punishment seeks to inflict pain in some sense on the wrongdoer and so could be condemned as an infringement of the offender's rights. Most obviously, prison infringes the fundamental human right to freedom.

While strictly irrelevant to those whose opposition is based on the fundamental belief that smacking violates basic human rights, arguments based on the consequences of smacking are also used:

- It is argued that smacking is a form of physical violence that damages children (physically and/or psychologically), even if that is not the intention of the parent.
- Children, it is claimed, also learn to respond to negative situations by recourse to physical violence if their parents smack them when they do something wrong. This is, in short, another example of violence that in turn begets more violence.
- Finally, it is alleged that there is little evidence that smacking is an effective form of deterrent or correction. In contrast, it is argued that other forms of punishment are better able to meet the goals a parent should have in the discipline of children.

Is, then, a viable defence of corporal punishment within the home possible when it is banned everywhere else? There are two central planks in the argument that it is sometimes right to smack:

- It is claimed that the distinctive nature of the parent–child relationship makes the administration of punishment within the family different from that in other contexts. This explains why a form of punishment may be acceptable here but not elsewhere. It is legitimate to treat children differently from adults because they are children. They need a particular form of discipline and training in right and wrong. Just as certain forms of affectionate physical contact are acceptable in the context of the home and a loving relationship between parent and child, so certain forms of punitive physical contact are appropriate that are not acceptable in other contexts.

● It is argued that in the context of loving care, careful explanation and forgiveness, controlled and limited physical pain can be an acceptable and an effective means of punishment. It both teaches a child to avoid physical dangers and trains them not to do certain seriously wrong actions (such as attacking their brother or sister). Indeed, some would argue that other forms of non-corporal punishment can be much more distressing for children.

Given the different moral views, the further question raised is the relation of the law to smacking: should it be illegal? All are agreed that children must be protected from abuse but whether all corporal punishment is equivalent to abuse remains disputed. It is also clearly quite consistent to believe smacking is wrong and not to smack your own children but also to believe that parents should not be prosecuted for smacking. Recent legislation has sought to tighten the law without making all smacking a crime. The difficult questions raised by arguments about legislation in this area are how to determine the boundary lines and how best to police them. In addition, punishing parents – particularly by imprisonment – inevitably has an effect on their children. It may be that in some cases the negative effect on a child's welfare of prosecuting their parent is even greater than the negative effect of the parent's corporal punishment.

Capital punishment

Many extreme forms of punishment can be inflicted on convicted criminals but the most extreme is that which ends their life. Can the taking of a human life ever be justified as a form of punishment? For most of human history this was not a controversial ethical subject. Capital punishment was an accepted norm. Debate focused on the crimes to which it should be applied and what form execution should take. In ancient Israel, the Old Testament Mosaic Law lists over 30 capital offences, including not just murder but idolatry, magic, blasphemy, violation of the sabbath, adultery and bestiality. The forms of execution used are also diverse: burning, decapitation, stoning and strangulation.

It is only in the last three decades that opposition to the death penalty has become widespread and effective. In 1977 only 16 countries had abolished capital punishment for all crimes. By 2004 over 80 countries had done so. A further 40 countries have effectively ended capital punishment in practice, leaving about 75 countries that continue to use it. Since 1997 the United Nations Commission on Human Rights has annually called for all states to stop executions even if they retain capital punishment on the statute book. Although figures are difficult to validate, it is reckoned that in 2004 over 7,000 people were sentenced to death in over 60 countries and nearly 4,000 people were actually executed (in 25 different countries). Perhaps even more shocking is that just 4 countries – China, Iran, Vietnam and the US – are reckoned to account for 97 per cent of state executions.

In the UK the last people to be executed by hanging were two men who were convicted of murder in 1964. Before that date over 800 people had been executed in the course of the twentieth century. In 1965 a five-year experimental abolition was started and this was later reaffirmed and finally made permanent throughout the UK in 1973. There were, however, some exceptions (such as treason and piracy with violence) and it was not until 1999 that the government signed the Sixth Protocol of the European Convention on Human Rights and formally and fully abolished the death penalty. Despite this relatively long-standing rejection of capital punishment and repeated failures to reverse its abolition in parliament, there remains widespread popular support (probably a majority according to many opinion polls) for reintroducing the death penalty.

Many of the arguments for and against the death penalty can be sketched by referring back to the four different goals related to punishment that were discussed earlier.

The moral order

For many advocates of the death penalty the fundamental rationale is that certain crimes – most obviously murder – are so serious that death is a legitimate penal response to those who are guilty. Some find support for this view in the biblical text, 'Whoever sheds the blood of man, by man shall his blood be shed; for in the image of God has God made man' (Genesis 9:6). Any lesser punishment, they might argue, denies the severity of the offence. Those who defend this view argue that the recent rejection of the death penalty is in part due to a contemporary dislike of retribution in punishment and a lack of belief in a transcendent moral order that the state serves. It is, however, quite possible to affirm the importance of retribution and oppose the death penalty as a disproportionate and unnecessary measure. Jesus' saying, 'You have heard that it was said, "Eye for eye, and tooth for tooth." But I tell you, do not resist an evil person. If someone strikes you on the right cheek, turn to him the other also' (Matthew 5:38–39), can be said to reject any simple equivalence that might support the view that a murderer should be executed.

The victim

Perhaps the strongest reason for continued popular support for the death penalty is that many sympathize with the desire for vindication on the part of the victim and their family. The loved ones of someone who has been brutally murdered cry out for justice and often their claim is that, for the punishment to fit the crime, capital punishment must be available. The biblical story of the first murder illustrates this social phenomenon: Abel's blood cries out from the ground (Genesis 4:10) and Cain worries that 'whoever finds me will kill me' (Genesis 4:14). It is, however, important that God seeks to prevent such a cycle of revenge. He places a mysterious mark on Cain that offered him, even as the murderer of his brother, divine protection. This restraint is also evident in Jesus' own handling of an alleged capital offence in the story of the woman caught in adultery (John 8). Here his famous words 'Let him who is without sin cast the first stone' lead to the dispersal of the executioners and, many have argued, should make all of us refrain from calling for a criminal's death.

The offender

The strongest argument against the death penalty is obviously that it is incapable of rehabilitating the criminal as it ends his or her life. For many, particularly those for whom this aspect of punishment is dominant, this argument is decisive. Through most of Western history, however, belief in life after death meant this claim was not as powerful. In fact, the fear of facing God's judgment after execution was a powerful force that led many people to conversion. That phenomenon continues today with reports of life-changing experiences on death row. More famous recent examples include the cases of William Payton and Carla Faye Tucker, whose claims to have become born-again Christians led to attempts to have their death sentences commuted to life imprisonment.

Society

Perhaps the most contentious area of debate concerns whether capital punishment is effective in protecting society. Clearly it effectively removes any future threat posed by the executed criminal. In some societies it may perhaps be the only way of doing this, and that is why some are cautious about judging capital punishment to be wrong at all times and in all places. However, in most modern societies other forms of punishment (notably highly secure imprisonment) offer sufficient protection for the death of the offender to be unnecessary. What remains much more hotly debated is whether capital punishment has a deterrent effect on others and so reduces serious crime. The experience of countries that have abolished capital punishment suggests abolition does not lead to an increase in previously capital crimes. It is certainly clear from the American experience that the death penalty exists alongside widespread violent crime. Indeed, some have argued that the maintenance of the death penalty perpetuates a wider culture of death rather than acting as a restraint on potential criminals.

A final argument, but one that fits none of these four categories, is decisive for many in this debate – namely the risk and consequences of human error. Even in relatively incorrupt judicial systems, innocent people are sometimes convicted for crimes they did not commit. Such rough justice is always a serious problem, but when the punishment is death there is no way the defendant can benefit from any redress of the error. Such errors are perhaps particularly common in cases where the crimes in question arouse great public outcry and there is a desire to secure a conviction. In the UK, since the ending of the death penalty, there have been a number of miscarriages of justice, for example, the Guildford Four, the Birmingham Six, the Tottenham Three, the Bridgewater Four. These could have led to executions if capital punishment was still in place. Four people who were hanged in the 1950s (most famously Derek Bentley whose story was told in the film *Let Him Have It*) have subsequently had their convictions judged 'unsafe', and many reckon an even larger number of earlier convictions may have led to the death of innocent or mentally ill people.

Through most of Christian history, most Christians have accepted or even supported the death penalty. A particularly important biblical text was the thirteenth chapter of Paul's letter to the Romans, which speaks of God ordaining political authority and granting it to the sword to punish wrongdoing. This has been read as authorizing the state to use, in certain circumstances, the ultimate punishment in fulfilling its God-given task of pursuing justice. Increasingly however, the church – including the pope – has been critical of capital punishment. It has come to be viewed at best as practically unnecessary in modern society (and so efforts should be made to abandon it) and at worst as intrinsically immoral and so to be opposed in principle.

Conclusion

In one of his most powerful plays which reflects on the practice of judgment and punishment, Shakespeare includes the memorable words, 'Though justice be thy plea, consider this, That, in the course of justice, none of us should see salvation.' Rather than focusing on justice and just punishment, Portia instead extols the qualities of mercy: 'It is an attribute to God himself; And earthly power doth then show likest God's When mercy seasons justice.' Punishment, as we have seen, is a necessary and universal feature of human experience. That is because wrongdoing is a universal feature of human experience. The danger – especially when we are the one who has been hurt – is that we view punishment as unproblematic or, worse still, seek rigorous and harsh, or even 'cruel and unusual', punishments, especially in the face of extreme wrongs. Part of the task of ethics is therefore critically to evaluate particular regimes of punishment, as this chapter has done in relation to smacking and state executions. The deeper ethical challenge in any society, especially for Christians who have known God's own merciful judgment in Christ, is to recall the wisdom of Portia's words and to seek ways, when administering justice and using any earthly systems of punishment, to moderate the penalties inflicted and display mercy.

8. Animals

Throughout much of human history, the ethics of how we treat animals was not a matter of major philosophical or political concern. Recently all that has changed, with awareness of these issues increasing significantly. Major philosophers such as Peter Singer are writing on the subject of animal liberation, and popular movements campaign for changes in British laws and attitudes to animals. Before examining three areas of dispute – eating animals, experimenting on animals and hunting animals – it is necessary to understand why there has been such a shift in recent decades. Only when we are clear about the different views that exist on this topic and about the general obligations humans have to animals can we understand differences over specific ethical issues concerning their treatment.

Traditional views of animals

The reason that animals have not been prominent in ethical debate for most of Western history is that both Christian and ancient classical understandings supported a strong sense of hierarchy between humans and animals. Animals were viewed as being largely at the free disposal of humans. This was reaffirmed during the Enlightenment by its emphasis on reason as a defining feature of humanity. Some, however, are now questioning that way of looking at the world, even claiming that certain animals have a higher moral status than certain humans.

Clearly there is both continuity and discontinuity between humans and animals; we share much in common but we are also significantly different. Disagreements arise over just how morally significant these differences are.

The ancient Greek philosopher Aristotle defended a clear hierarchy within creation – plants existing for the sake of animals and animals in turn existing for the sake of humans. In such a framework, animals exist simply to serve human interests and desires. They have no significant moral status of their own. As long as it serves some human good, causing animals harm or destroying them should not be considered ethically questionable. From this viewpoint, there is really no significant moral debate about eating, hunting or experimenting on animals.

A similar hierarchical and instrumental perspective of the relationship between humans and animals developed within mainstream Christian thinking and appealed to the Bible for its views. The biblical creation accounts clearly privilege humanity within God's creation: men and women are the pinnacle of God's creation and are uniquely 'made in the image of God' (Genesis 1:27). God also gives humans a role in relation to animals: 'Let them rule over the fish of the sea and the birds of the air, over the livestock, over all the earth, and over all the creatures that move along the ground' (Genesis 1:26, 28). As a result, most leading Christian theologians down through the centuries have taken a view similar to that of Augustine, who argued that irrational animals are subjected to rational humans to be used as they see fit.

In modern times, the influence of Enlightenment thinking also led to a clear and qualitative distinction being upheld which also focused on rationality. The seventeenth-century philosopher

René Descartes' famous dictum, 'I think, therefore I am', highlights the importance of rational thought and the possession of a mind. Animals, lacking these qualities, were therefore to be viewed as little more than animate machines and their welfare was deemed to be of little moral significance.

Rethinking the tradition

A number of different factors have led to a re-evaluation of this traditional way of viewing the animal kingdom, although its rationale is not always clearly articulated or understood. The following three factors in particular have contributed in different ways to the questioning of the traditional view and have led to the treatment of animals being increasingly recognized as an important ethical issue.

Evolution

As a result of widespread acceptance of the theory of human evolution from animals, the gap between humans and animals has appeared to be much less significant than it perhaps did to those who read Genesis literally and so emphasized the special creation of humanity. Our common bond with the rest of the animal kingdom – particularly primates – has led to a rethink concerning claims about the unique and qualitatively superior status of humans.

Stewardship

Christians have also begun to question whether the traditional understanding of creation failed to recognize the importance of non-human creation to God and therefore the significance of human responsibilities to animals. It is argued that the mandate that God gives to humans in Genesis 1:28 to 'rule over the fish of the sea and the birds of the air and over every living creature that moves along the ground' should not be understood in terms of dominance, control and disposal but rather in terms of care and stewardship – the sort of rule Christians believe is seen in Jesus Christ. There are also many signs of God's care and concern for animals ranging from their protection in Noah's ark (Genesis 9) to the remarkable last verse of the book of Jonah, where God defends his preservation of Nineveh by stating that 'Nineveh has more than a hundred and twenty thousand people who cannot tell their right hand from their left, and many cattle as well' (Jonah 4:11). In the Bible's vision of the end of time, the renewed creation is a peaceable kingdom that includes animals as well as humans, as in Isaiah's prophecy that the wolf will live with the lamb (Isaiah 11:6–9). Furthermore, rather than viewing them as simply being at the disposal of humans, Psalm 50 makes clear God's concern for and ownership of animals: '… every animal of the forest is mine, and the cattle on a thousand hills. I know every bird in the mountains, and the creatures of the field are mine' (Psalm 50:10–11). In the light of this wider biblical picture, it is argued that many Christians have developed distorted understandings of the relationship between humans and animals. It has also been recognized that within Christian tradition there are those who are marked by a different outlook from the dominant one and by their care for animals. Most famous here, of course, is St Francis of Assisi, the patron saint of animals.

Suffering

'The question is not, can they *reason*? Nor can they *talk*? But, can they *suffer*?' These words of the late-eighteenth and nineteenth-century English philosopher Jeremy Bentham capture a fundamental shift that has taken place in how we think about the treatment of animals. Rather than viewing them as fundamentally different from us because of their lack of reason and verbal communication, the shared animal and human experience of pain and suffering has become central to many people's understanding. It is argued that animals have interests that we must recognize and respect because they, like us, are sentient creatures (unlike stones or cars for example). They have a capacity to suffer and to experience pleasure. The exact nature of animal pain and suffering is, of course, an area of much debate, but it is now widely held that much traditional thinking about animals was fundamentally flawed in failing to incorporate this fact into its understanding. Some go further to argue that on the basis of animals' sentience we can speak of (at least some) animals having desires, preferences and thus a form of mental life.

New ways of thinking: speciesism and animal rights

These changes in thinking have led to the development of a whole new framework for addressing ethical questions about our treatment of animals. Two new moral categories are of particular importance in understanding this: speciesism and animal rights.

We are now increasingly aware of the reality of racism, sexism and various other patterns of belief and behaviour that represent unjust and often unconscious prejudice and discrimination. All of these are based on divisions we make between people. But some ethicists have asked why we should limit our moral categories in this way. After all, how would we feel if a more intelligent species were to come to earth and inflict suffering and pain on us, using us purely for their benefit, and then defend their actions on the grounds that we were a different and inferior species?

The term 'speciesism' was coined in 1970 by Richard Ryder. Ryder is a British psychologist who abandoned animal experiments and became a leading thinker in this area, urging us to reconsider how we viewed and treated animals. Speciesism is the negative term used for the view that, simply because something belongs to a different species, this justifies different treatment and patterns of behaviour that would be considered immoral if performed in relation to any fellow humans – even those whose abilities (for example, of communication or mobility) may be no better than that of some animals.

One way of thinking that underlies speciesism is that animals, like humans, can be said to have rights and that we often disregard these animal rights in the way we treat them. As there is considerable philosophical debate about what it means even for humans to have rights (for example, the nature, origin and content of such rights), what it means for animals to have rights is, unsurprisingly, an even more contentious subject. Critics may ridicule the idea (asking whether penguins have the right to vote) or, more seriously, they may question how animals gain such rights or can possibly claim them. The central argument, however, is that on the basis of morally relevant characteristics that animals share with humans (for example, the ability to suffer), they are owed certain things by humans that we acknowledge to be rights for our fellow men and women but which we regularly deny animals.

These different ways of viewing animals inevitably shape different ethical responses to particular issues concerning our treatment of animals. The rest of this chapter sketches some of the arguments for and against vegetarianism, animal experimentation and hunting.

Eating animals

Most of the time, most of us give little thought to the morality of what we eat. Yet a different diet will have a major effect on animals. The old story of the chicken suggesting to the pig that they cheer up some miserable humans by offering them an egg and bacon breakfast sums it up well: 'I'm not sure I like that idea,' replies the pig. 'It just requires a contribution from you, from me it demands quite a commitment!' The level of that commitment on animals is huge: it is estimated that the number of animals killed for food is over 20 billion a year in the US and 2.5 million a day in the UK alone.

Alongside the growing intellectual debate about our treatment of animals there has been a rapid rise in the number of vegetarians. In the UK it is reckoned that around 7 per cent of people are now vegetarians, with women much more likely to be non-meat eaters than men. Children are increasingly becoming vegetarians, perhaps due to such powerful influences as the film *Babe* and Roald Dahl's provocative poem 'The Pig', which is about a clever pig who, when he realizes that 'The butcher's shop! The carving knife! That is the reason for my life!', turns on the farmer. The pig kills him and eats him; 'And when he finished, Pig, of course, Felt absolutely no remorse. Slowly he scratched his brainy head And with a little smile he said, "I had a fairly powerful hunch That he might have me for his lunch. And so, because I feared the worst, I thought I'd better eat him first."'

Some of the reasons for not eating meat are not based on

moral considerations but on matters of personal taste or health concerns. There is, however, also a strong ethical rationale offered for not eating meat.

Clearly if it is held that animals have rights then presumably they have the most basic of rights – a right to life, a right not to be killed. From this perspective, there may perhaps be contexts in which animal killing is justifiable if humans are to survive. However, in relation to human food needs today, this is clearly not the case in most of the world because other suitable food is available. Killing animals to eat them is, therefore, an unjustifiable denial of the animal's right to life.

Others argue that even if killing animals for food could be justified, the treatment of animals bred for food (though rarely considered by those who purchase their Sunday joint in the supermarket) is cruel. In order to reduce costs and meet the mass market for meat, a form of factory farming has developed in which animals are herded into large warehouses and kept in small cages until they are slaughtered. The processes by which animals are prepared for our dinner plates – for example, de-beaking chickens, castrating pigs – pay no regard to the pain and suffering that the animal experiences. Whether or not meat-eating can be justified in theory, the argument is that in reality to buy and eat meat products produced in this way is to support and perpetuate this system of suffering.

Meat-eating is such a standard way of life that most non-vegetarians give little thought to the moral questions it raises. Most of those who defend meat-eating do so because they are unconvinced by the claims of 'animal rights' and maintain a sense that animals exist to serve human needs, including the needs of their taste buds. While there may be concerns about cruelty in some food production, this need not mean refusing to eat all meat. Free-range meat products, for example, might be preferred. It is also argued that many animals today only have a life because of their place in the food industry and that, given they will all die anyway, there is no great wrong done in determining when their life will end so that they can be enjoyed as food by humans.

Some Christians will also claim biblical warrant for eating animals. Although it appears that Adam and Eve were expected to be vegetarians, eating only plants (Genesis 1:29), God allows humans to eat meat after the Flood (Genesis 9:3). Vegetarianism is never explicitly commanded for Jews or Christians in scripture, nor is it prominent in Christian tradition. Indeed, in a famous story in which God challenges the apostle Peter's views about non-Jews, he does so by commanding him to kill and eat animals he had previously considered unclean (Acts 10). For most people – Christian and non-Christian – the issue of meat-eating is therefore still seen (rightly or wrongly) more as a matter of personal taste than one of moral significance.

Experimenting on animals

For many people, a word association game with the word 'beagle' would lead to such unusual responses as 'smoking', 'pipe' or 'cigarette'. The reason, of course, is the role that experiments on these dogs has played in debates about the health risks of tobacco for humans. Images of smoking dogs became prominent and almost symbolic in debates about the use of animals in research. More recently, the issues of the use of animals in scientific experiments were captured in the astonishing photo of a mouse 'growing' a human ear on its back.

Throughout human history, humans have carried out

experiments on animals (often called 'vivisection') that would clearly be considered immoral were they to be done on humans. As long ago as the sixth century BC, the function of the optic nerve was demonstrated on live animals by cutting through these nerves to demonstrate that they became blind. Historically, many medical discoveries relating to the human body were made in the context of animal experimentation. Animals have also been used to test numerous new medical techniques and cures, from blood transfusion and insulin to organ transplants and polio vaccines. When, in the late nineteenth century, it became possible to use general anaesthetic to make animals unconscious, the number of animal experiments in the UK shot up from a few hundred in 1881 when records began to nearly 100,000 twenty years later. Through the twentieth century the numbers continued to soar, although they fell dramatically in the final decades due to popular protest and stricter legal controls. Nevertheless, in 2002, in the UK alone, there were over 2.7 million authorized experiments on live animals, most of which did not involve anaesthesia.

Clearly there is great variety within the broad category of 'animal experimentation' and ethical distinctions could be drawn in relation to a number of different issues.

The purpose of the experiment

Here different sub-categories can be defined. Some experiments are for medical research, some for product testing (for example, cosmetics) and some for military purposes – although even these divisions are not watertight. Most people will be much more sympathetic to experiments held to be necessary in order to find or test a cure for some serious disease than to those that are part of a development of a new luxury good.

The animal involved in the experiment

Those opposed to experiments tend to focus their publicity on animals that are popular pets (for example, rabbits and dogs) whereas most experiments – over 2 million in the UK – are carried out on mice and other rodents. Moral distinctions are difficult to defend based on the 'aaah' factor of sentiment towards particular species but other factors may be important. It is significant that in the UK no great apes can be used in experiments and testing on other primates raises most concern.

The level of suffering caused by the experiment

There is a great variety in the forms of test and the levels of pain inflicted on the animal, but in most cases the animal suffers to some (often significant) degree and is then killed at the end of the process.

The value of the experiment

The other important criterion is of course the value of the experiment itself. Here there are two factors. First, the benefits that will arise if the experiment succeeds in providing the information sought. These could range from knowing the effectiveness of a new drug to finding out how animals react under duress. This is something that can be known in advance and so some form of cost–benefit analysis could be applied to see if the benefits of success would outweigh the costs involved. Second, and much more difficult to determine, is whether the experiment will succeed in its goal. It may well inflict suffering but yield no results or only provide results that are not applicable to humans.

For those most committed to animal rights and fighting speciesism such distinctions will be of little or no practical importance. They will campaign for the ending of all experimentation that causes pain or death to animals. Some, such as Richard Ryder, were previously involved in vivisection but came to be revolted by the whole practice and by the pain – in some cases effectively torture – inflicted on animals. This, they argue, is done because of what they see as humanity's almost religious commitment to scientific advance and commercial and military interests. The abolition of such experiments is, from such a perspective, a moral duty and absolute. While attempts can be made to improve the situation by legal reform, many seek recourse to direct action. Most of those opposed have taken non-violent action such as seeking to liberate animals being bred or used for experiments. In recent years, however, more extreme supporters have even used violence against those humans involved in inflicting pain and suffering on animals in laboratories. Their logic parallels that of extreme anti-abortionists: those involved in such procedures are legitimate targets because they are involved in denying a creature's fundamental right to life.

Many people, while not opposing all vivisection, will be shocked at how cruel and unnecessary some experiments on animals can be. One common way of seeking to reduce and limit such procedures is know as the 3R's and this has been very influential in reform of legislation in this area. It calls for the replacement, reduction and refinement of existing forms of animal experimentation in order to make the process more humane and to combat cruelty.

The first R – *replacement* – issues a moral challenge to find alternative means of research that do not require animal suffering. It is important to recognize that already the overwhelming majority of medical research is not carried out on animals.

The second R does not strictly call for a *reduction* in the total number of animal experiments. Its concern is rather to reduce the number of animals used in any experiment to the bare minimum necessary to gain the required results.

The third R seeks to *refine* every experiment so that the level of pain and suffering is kept to the absolute minimum. It is reckoned that the overwhelming majority of experiments carried out on animals in the UK now inflict only mild (rather than moderate or substantial) suffering.

This moral framework therefore seeks to avoid excessive, disproportionate suffering but to accept that animal suffering in experiments is justifiable in certain situations.

Hunting animals

The other possible link most people would make with beagles is, paradoxically, that of hunting. This raises the third of our ethical issues related to animals. As with animal experimentation and meat-eating, hunting is another long-standing human practice that is increasingly being called into question as a result of new understandings of animals and their status in relation to humans. For many years now there has been growing hostility in the UK to the traditional 'hunting with hounds'. Following seven failed attempts to restrict or ban hunting with dogs since 1949, the activity was, after much debate and controversy, made illegal in almost all situations in the UK from November 2004.

Here again the underlying issues and disagreements already examined play a crucial part in the development of different perspectives. The strongest arguments against hunting come from those committed to animal rights for whom the lengthy pursuit and then killing of an animal for entertainment and sport is clearly cruel and unjustifiable. The practice represents an acceptance of (or even a delight in) the suffering and death of an animal. This is not a virtue but a vice, illuminating the viciousness of human beings. Even among many who would not take an absolutist position in favour of animal rights, most, if not all, forms of hunting that go beyond what is necessary for survival are, at best, morally ambiguous. This is because they inflict suffering and death on animals often with little or no apparent benefit to humans.

Advocates of hunting will, however, insist that hunting other animals is a perfectly natural phenomenon of the animal kingdom – which includes human beings – and is therefore not morally reprehensible. Furthermore, it is not as cruel to the fox as is often claimed, while a ban will require use of alternative means of pest control to replace it and to assist conservation. These other forms – for example, traps, gassing, shooting – often inflict more pain and suffering on the animals. Thus, even if hunting is an 'evil', it is a 'lesser evil'. It is also argued that great social and economic benefits result from the existence of hunts and that these will be lost with a ban, so animal welfare is being advanced at a cost to humans.

Conclusion

Space has prevented detailed examination of the data used to support different sides on these three contentious issues. It is, however, clear that the more fundamental causes of disagreement are philosophical. They relate to the status of animals within a wider understanding of the nature and distinctiveness of human beings. While few would now treat animal suffering as unimportant (let alone in any sense a good), the extent to which it should be considered 'bad' or 'evil' remains an area of major dispute. There is a growing realization that the distinction drawn between humans and other animals has, in the past, been too great. For some, almost any such distinction – particularly if it legitimates suffering or death – is a corrupt ideology (speciesism) equivalent to racism in its denial of fundamental rights. Those holding such a perspective will logically stand opposed in principle to vivisection and hunting and will be committed vegetarians. At the other end of the scale, some will see these issues of eating, experimenting on and hunting animals as of little or no moral significance because of their view of human supremacy. Increasingly, however, people are developing an attitude which may parallel that found in relation to other evils such as **war**. There is a desire to limit and control the pain and suffering humans can legitimately inflict on non-human creatures although considerable diversity of opinion remains over what constitutes a disproportionate cost and an unjustifiable pattern of human life.

9. Environment

Few who watched the scenes from New Orleans in September 2005 will forget the devastation wrought in the US by recent hurricanes Katrina and Rita. Those events have, perhaps, provided a timely reminder to the developed world. We have seen that even the most technologically advanced, wealthy and urban civilization cannot escape the fact that we humans are not in total control of our planet. We remain subject to natural forces and these can often be highly destructive.

Most of our choices and actions probably have a limited effect on many of these natural forces. However, we are increasingly aware that some human decisions do have an impact – especially when they become patterns of life that are embraced by whole societies and cultures. This effect may be for good or, perhaps more often, our choices may do harm both to the world and ultimately to human beings. In the last 30 years or so, ethicists have become increasingly interested in environmental ethics and the ethical issues raised by human activity in relation to the non-human world. Some of the issues raised within this area were discussed in the chapter on **animals**. This chapter takes a wider frame of reference. It introduces some of the different ways of thinking about the environment and why they should matter ethically. It then examines just two of the many pressing environmental challenges: global warming and the development of genetically modified foods.

Why does the environment matter?

The first and most important issue that needs to be addressed is how we view the non-human world and why it might be considered a serious ethical concern. As we have seen in other chapters, here again there are various deeper worldviews and perspectives. These, in turn, lead to differing approaches to specific ethical challenges. Broadly speaking, three different ways of approaching this area can be distinguished on the basis of what is central to each framework – whether it is human beings (anthropocentric), the earth as a whole (geocentric) or God (theocentric).

Anthropocentric perspectives

The very term we commonly use – 'environment' – reflects the fact that most people in Western history and today view the world with humans at the centre. The rest of the planet is secondary and, to some degree, peripheral – it is simply *our* environment. Aristotle commented that 'nature has made all things specifically for the sake of man', and this has been the predominant outlook ever since. This means that while animals and trees and seas have been seen as having some value it has generally been an *instrumental* value. They are of value, in other words, because they are means to an end and provide humans with resources (for example, food or minerals or natural medicines). Unlike human beings they are not held to have *intrinsic* value, value in their own right and as ends in themselves.

In a famous article in 1967 the historian Professor Lynn White argued that such anthropocentrism arose largely because 'especially in its Western form, Christianity is the most anthropocentric religion the world has seen'. He concluded that the historical roots of the ecological crisis had to be understood theologically and were due at least in part to Christianity. White highlighted the Christian view that man was made in 'the image of God' and claimed that, as a result of this understanding, Christians viewed humans as sharing much of God's transcendence over nature. Christianity 'not only established a dualism of man and nature but also insisted that it is God's will that man exploit nature for his proper ends'. This particular form of anthropocentricism led, it was claimed, to attitudes and patterns of behaviour that despoiled and exploited the natural world. White and his followers argued that this image of humans as god-like rulers over the world helped to create the ecological crisis which, by the late 1960s and early 1970s, people were already beginning to realize was a reality.

More recently, anthropocentric arguments have been developed in order to encourage more care for the environment. These represent a sort of enlightened or prudential anthropocentric outlook in which humans take a longer-term but still self-interested outlook. They recognize that what we do to the environment often ultimately has effects on the human race as well. It may be true, for example, that we can pollute our air and water with only minimal concern regarding its effects on us as individuals (though even that is now a less persuasive argument). Nevertheless, it is argued, we have a responsibility to future generations of human beings who will be affected by the state in which we leave the planet for them to live on. From this consequentialist perspective, there may be incentives for judging certain actions wrong and refraining from them because of their effect on our children and grandchildren. What is important is that this is still not because of what they do to non-humans (which remains of little importance) but because of their longer-term effects on fellow humans who remain at the centre of the world.

Geocentric perspectives

Such environmentally-aware, consequentialist but still human-centred approaches to our treatment of the natural world have been challenged by thinkers who wish to remove humanity from centre-stage dominance and give intrinsic value to non-humans. To show concern about pollution simply because of its effects on the standard of life of human beings has been dismissed by some as 'shallow ecology'. In its place they proposed 'deep ecology'. Partly out of appreciation for non-Christian religions that recognized the sacredness of mountains and other natural phenomena, those who developed this outlook began to emphasize what was called 'biospheric egalitarianism'. This held that all things have intrinsic value in their own right without regard to the benefit they might bring to human beings. In the early 1970s, the thinker most associated with this movement, Arne Naess, produced the Deep Ecology Platform. This laid out the following eight principles for thinking about the environment and our human relationship to it.

> 1. The well-being and flourishing of human and non-human life on Earth have value in themselves (synonyms: inherent worth; intrinsic value; inherent value). These values are independent of the usefulness of the non-human world for human purposes.
> 2. Richness and diversity of life forms contribute to the realization of these values and are also values in themselves.

3. Humans have no right to reduce this richness and diversity except to satisfy vital needs.

4. Present human interference with the non-human world is excessive, and the situation is rapidly worsening.

5. The flourishing of human life and cultures is compatible with a substantial decrease of the human population. The flourishing of non-human life requires such a decrease.

6. Policies must therefore be changed. The changes in policies affect basic economic, technological structures. The resulting state of affairs will be deeply different from the present.

7. The ideological change is mainly that of appreciating life quality (dwelling in situations of inherent worth) rather than adhering to an increasingly higher standard of living. There will be a profound awareness of the difference between big and great.

8. Those who subscribe to the foregoing points have an obligation directly or indirectly to participate in the attempt to implement the necessary changes.

An even more elaborate form of geocentric understanding is represented by the concept of Gaia (named after the Greek goddess of the earth). This comes in many forms – some more explicitly spiritual and mystical than others – the most important of which was first developed by the scientist James Lovelock. This perspective views the earth as a whole as a 'self-regulating entity with the capacity to keep our planet healthy by controlling the chemical and physical environment'. The earth is, therefore, greater than any of its individual parts, including the human. Lovelock's central thesis is that 'if we see the world as a superorganism of which we are a part – not the owner, nor the tenant, not even a passenger – we could have a long time ahead of us and our species might survive for its "alloted span" '.

Those who view the world from this geocentric outlook will probably interpret the evidence differently and will certainly draw ethical conclusions that differ significantly from any of the anthropocentric ways of thinking about the natural world.

Theocentric perspectives

A significant number of Christians have felt challenged to address the environmental crisis and in particular to respond to the claims of Lynn White and his followers that the influence of the Bible and Christian theology bear a considerable responsibility for it. At the heart of the challenge to Christian thinking is the interpretation of the Genesis creation narrative, with its clear privileging of humanity and in particular the command to 'have dominion' over other animals and the earth (Genesis 1:26) and to 'fill the earth and subdue it' (Genesis 1:28). However, as White himself acknowledged, Christian history was not monochrome but quite varied in its attitudes. In fact, few Christian theologians could be accused of reading these verses as a divine warrant for human 'domination' or 'exploitation' of non-human creation.

In much recent Christian environmental thinking a central theme is that both the Genesis account and other parts of scripture show humans to be 'stewards' who are called to care for God's creation and who are ultimately accountable to him for their use and abuse of it. Here, although there may be a soft form of anthropocentricism (in that humans have a central and distinctive calling), it is ultimately God who is at the centre.

One example of this outlook is the 1994 Evangelical

Declaration on the Care of Creation. This takes as its biblical text the words of the Psalmist, 'The earth is the Lord's, and the fullness thereof' (Psalm 24:1). The declaration opens by affirming that 'because we worship and honour the Creator, we seek to cherish and care for creation' but then confesses 'we have failed in our stewardship of creation… we have polluted, distorted or destroyed so much of the Creator's work'. Importantly – and in contrast to much Christian thinking (but not the Bible) – it applies God's work of redemption to the whole of creation. It speaks of the need 'to extend Christ's healing to suffering creation' and looks forward to 'the time when even the groaning creation will be restored to wholeness' because 'in Christ there is hope, not only for men, women and children, but also for the rest of creation which is suffering from the consequences of human sin'.

This offers yet another framework for thinking about the environment. It recognizes humanity's special position and role but without thereby viewing humans almost as despots in sovereign control of the planet. Instead, human failures are acknowledged and limits recognized. So the declaration lists seven degradations of creation (land degradation, deforestation, species extinction, water degradation, global toxification, the alteration of atmosphere, and human and cultural degradation) which 'are signs that we are pressing against the finite limits God has set for creation'. Even more importantly, this Christian vision offers a hope that does not depend ultimately on human activity even though it calls for all of us to care for the planet.

Having sketched these three ways of thinking about our relationship to the environment, the rest of this chapter focuses on two of the most contentious contemporary areas of ethical concern: global warming and climate change, and genetic modification of crops.

Global warming and climate change

It is currently estimated by scientists that, over the next hundred years, average temperatures on the earth will rise by between 1.5 and 6 degrees centigrade and global sea levels by anything from 9 cm to 90 cm. The seriousness of this becomes evident when set against the fact that today's temperatures are only 0.6 degrees hotter than a century ago and, because average global temperatures have fluctuated by less than 1 degree since the dawn of civilization, the earth is now only 4 to 5 degrees warmer than it was during the Ice Age.

It is generally accepted that one of the main reasons for this change in climate is the effect of certain human actions on the atmosphere, commonly known as the 'greenhouse effect'. The greenhouse effect is the natural process by which the atmosphere traps solar energy and warms the earth. What is changing is that the emission of 'greenhouse gases' such as carbon dioxide (through actions such as burning fossil fuels and deforestation) is helping to increase this greenhouse effect and so to create global warming. The level of change is fairly clear. Before the Industrial Revolution, atmospheric concentrations of carbon dioxide were about 270–280 parts per million (ppm). They have now risen to stand at approximately 380 ppm, and in recent years they have been rising by about 1.5 ppm annually. What is less clear are the implications of these developments.

Much uncertainty exists as to the likely impact of these predicted changes both on the wider ecosystem and on humans. The extent of the changes is, however, so great that in 2004 the government's chief scientific adviser, Sir David King, warned that climate change presented a bigger threat to the planet than international terrorism. Among the possible effects are: greater water shortage in regions where water is already scarce; changes in weather patterns (some of which we may already be witnessing in more heatwaves, storms and droughts); and the extinction of various species. The effect of some of these developments in the poorest areas of the world could make the battle against **poverty** even more difficult – a reminder that environmental issues impact on wider social and political concerns.

Faced with these and other environmental challenges, the United Nations held the Earth Summit (officially the Conference on Environment and Development) in Brazil in 1992. This began to raise general awareness of the risks presented by climate change and other developments. Following this summit, and building on its initial agreements, the Kyoto Protocol was agreed in 1997. This seeks to set targets for the reduction of greenhouse gas emissions in industrialized countries and to monitor emissions in developing countries (some of which, such as China and India, are major producers of emissions). The stated goal is that by 2008–12 combined emissions will be cut by 5 per cent from their 1990 level, with different signatory countries agreeing their contribution to this target. By February 2005 the protocol had gained sufficient signatories to become a legally binding treaty (in fact 129 countries have now signed). A major problem, however, is that the US – responsible alone for about a quarter of all greenhouse gas emissions on the planet – and Australia have refused to sign the treaty.

Initially, there were promising signs of success with emissions falling overall by about 3 per cent in the last decade of the twentieth century. However, since then they have risen again sharply. The United Nations has warned that, far from reducing emissions, by 2010 the fact is that they will be 10 per cent higher than they were in 1990. Even more disconcerting is that many scientists estimate that the original targets would have minimal effect even if they were achieved. This is because they now believe that cuts as high as 60 per cent are needed if the worst effects of global warming are to be avoided.

It is governments who make agreements to cut greenhouse gas emissions, and most of these agreements will be implemented by controls on businesses (for example, it is estimated that by 2030 aircraft could cause 25 per cent of the UK's contribution to greenhouse gas emissions) and by finding alternative energy resources (some are now looking to nuclear power). It is clear, however, that the cumulative effect of small individual actions also contributes to global warming. Campaigning groups such as Friends of the Earth and Greenpeace therefore call for environmentally-aware decisions by individuals alongside strong legal commitments by governments. Each person can, by avoiding energy wastage, reducing car use and making other 'small-scale' contributions, do something to reduce the global warming problem. Here – as with shopping for Fairtrade goods to help combat poverty – there is a reminder that our simple everyday activities affect important global ethical issues.

Genetically modified food

In July 1999, Lord Melchett, along with over 25 fellow Greenpeace activists, invaded a six-and-a-half acre field in Norwich in order to destroy its crop of genetically modified maize. Despite admitting this before the court they were found not guilty of criminal damage by a jury in September 2000. This was a sure sign that popular opinion either shared their outright hostility to the development of genetically modified (GM) food or at least remained highly sceptical about such new technologies. Popular media stories of 'Frankenstein food' undoubtedly fuelled fears and concerns about these latest developments. Despite this, GM (or transgenic) crops are already grown by millions of farmers in over a dozen countries around the world.

Before sketching the main arguments advanced both for and against genetic modification of crops and other foods, it is helpful to clarify exactly what is involved in this scientific development. It is the application to non-human species of some of the science of genetic engineering discussed in relation to humans in the chapter on **genetics**. In general popular usage, the term 'GM food' incorporates a wide range of products, including all foods that have, at some stage, experienced genetic modification to produce something that does not appear naturally. This may be the food itself or ingredients that go into the food, even if they are then processed in such a way as to be indistinguishable from non-GM ingredients. 'GM food' would therefore include creating slow-softening tomatoes to give them a longer shelf life and enhancing rice to increase its iron levels or vitamin A content so that it might help combat disease.

The following arguments are given in favour of genetic modification.

Cost

There is evidence that the costs of GM crops may be less than natural crops. This comes both from those developing GM crops and from more neutral sources. For example, the 2003 report of the Prime Minister's Strategy Unit concluded that 'GM crops could offer some cost and convenience advantages to UK farmers now', and further stated that 'future developments in

GM crops have the potential to offer more wide-ranging benefits both to farmers and consumers'.

Help for poor countries
In addition, it has been argued that genetic modification could lead to increasing yields and so benefit poor countries and help to combat hunger. In December 2003, the Nuffield Council on Bioethics reported that GM crops could help address both agricultural problems (such as drought and salty soil) and health problems in developing countries.

Health benefits
Some forms of modification can bring health benefits, for example removing elements in food that can lead to allergies or illness in some consumers.

No known health risks
Rather than focusing on potential health benefits through genetic modification, most concern has been expressed about the health risks connected with GM foods. While it is obviously impossible to give absolute assurances, it is important to recognize that in March 2004, while calling for ongoing research, the British Medical Association confirmed that it shared the view of the Royal Society that 'that there is no robust evidence to prove that GM foods are unsafe'.

Arguments against genetic modification include:

Damage to non-GM crops
One of the central concerns of Lord Melchett and his fellow activists was that any production of GM crops would

contaminate non-GM crops within a large surrounding area. Both Friends of the Earth and a government report have found evidence of such cross-contamination. Groups such as the Soil Association claim this shows that permitting GM crops effectively results in discrimination against those seeking to produce GM-free food.

No necessary benefit for developing countries

Among the critics of GM developments are groups such as Oxfam and Christian Aid. They argue that, although there may be some benefits resulting from GM crops, the problems underlying world hunger will not be solved by developing them. In fact, by making poor populations reliant on large companies producing such crops, this development could further weaken local producers in the poorest countries.

Benefits biotechnology companies

Far from helping the poorest, it is argued that the widespread use of GM foods increases the power of the large companies (such as Monsanto) who hold the patents on seeds.

Health and environmental risks unknown

The claim here is that, with the technology still at such a relatively early stage, it is far from clear what the effects of widespread development of GM foods would be. There is some evidence that there may be risks both to the health of humans and to biodiversity.

Overall it is clear that there is still much uncertainty and even hostility towards the development and widespread availability of genetically modified crops and other GM foods. Undoubtedly some of this antagonism is fuelled by ignorance about **genetics** (leading to the 'yuk factor' at new developments) and by fears that this is another case in which ultimately human interference with the natural environment can only have negative effects. On the other hand, it can be argued that such genetic modification simply represents, at a new level of technological expertise, what humans have always done through selective breeding and that there is no evidence that these new techniques create major risks either to human well-being or to that of the planet as a whole.

Conclusion

The list of environmental challenges we face at the start of the twenty-first century is, of course, much greater than it has been possible to discuss here. In addition to climate change and genetic modification of crops there is the real threat of a new level of mass extinctions within the animal kingdom, the effect of pollution on both humans and other creatures, the threatened rise in water scarcity and the consequences of large-scale deforestation in countries such as Brazil. There is also the reality that, as already noted, concerns about the environment often relate to the challenge of **poverty**. For example, should the poorer countries be prevented from repeating the environmentally damaging policies pursued for many decades by developed countries even if by limiting them in this way to protect the environment they are forced to remain economically disadvantaged?

Perhaps the deepest challenge here is that, while increasing numbers of people in wealthy nations are becoming aware that their way of life is taking a toll on the planet that is ultimately not sustainable, the implications of changing that way of life are themselves very costly. Any serious attempt to reduce the damage we are doing to the planet will require a fundamental rethinking of the generally accepted pattern of life in the West. It will entail a pattern of self-discipline – even self-denial – and a way of living that keeps within limits that are not of our choosing. That stands in stark contrast to the consumerist, desire-fulfilling lifestyle that shapes both policy-making on the part of our governments and our own individual choices. It is perhaps this deeper issue rather than specific responses to individual environmental issues that represents the ultimate ethical challenge in relation to the environment.

10. Asylum and Immigration

In February 2005, with speculation mounting that a general election was imminent, the opinion pollsters MORI asked their regular questions seeking to identify what the electorate saw as the important issues facing Britain. Top of the poll, for the first time in its history, was 'race relations/immigration/immigrants'. Of those polled, 23 per cent thought it the *most* important issue (the next highest figure was 13 per cent for both the NHS and for defence/foreign affairs/international terrorism), and 40 per cent gave it as one among other important issues. These figures represented a peak in a trend that began at the turn of the millennium. Before then the subject was rarely viewed as an important issue by more than 5 per cent of those interviewed. From 2000 onwards, however, it rarely dipped below 10 per cent and usually between one-quarter and one-third of those polled identified it as an important issue.

Myth and reality

The context of this renewed concern was undoubtedly greater media coverage of the issues surrounding asylum, refugees and immigration. Sometimes these were tragic stories such as the deaths of 21 Chinese cockle pickers in Morecambe Bay in February 2004 or the 58 Chinese men and women found suffocated to death in the back of a lorry at Dover in summer 2000. At other times they were stories about the rapid rise in applications for asylum or the alleged conduct of 'illegal immigrants' that fuelled fears of being 'swamped' by 'bogus' asylum seekers. Unsurprisingly, in 2002 MORI found that 85 per cent of people interviewed associated negative terms with media reporting of asylum issues. The general population is, however, also remarkably ill-informed about the reality of the situation.

- On average, people think 23 per cent of the world's refugees and asylum seekers are in the UK. The reality is difficult to judge but is probably less than 2 per cent.
- When asked what proportion of the British population were immigrants (in other words, born abroad), the average response was 21 per cent. The reality is about 7 per cent (only 16 per cent of those asked chose the correct range of 6–10 per cent in their answer).
- On average it was thought asylum seekers received £113 a week in benefits. The reality was around £37.

Although these examples show that there are some serious misconceptions about the reality of the situation in the UK, it cannot be disputed that there have been major changes in recent years.

- In the mid 1980s there were about 4,000 applicants for asylum each year. This rose in the 1990s to an average of about 35,000 per annum. In 2002, there were over 85,000 – a 20 per cent increase on the previous year – although since then numbers have been falling.
- In the 1960s and 1970s the number of people who left Britain was greater than the number who arrived as immigrants. Between 1971 and 2001 however the number of people living in Britain who were born outside the country rose from 2.4 million (4.5 per cent of the population) to 4.3 million (7.5 per cent).

● In summer 2005 it was reported that about 130,000 nationals from the ten new nations within the EU had applied to work in the UK in the last half of 2004, over half of them from Poland.

Before looking at some of the specific ethical issues raised in relation to asylum and immigration policy it is once again necessary to get a sense of the bigger picture. In this case that means clarifying what exactly we are talking about and then setting the British situation in a global context.

Understanding the terms

One of the real problems affecting much discussion of this topic is that terms are often used without great care and with little clarity. Whether this is intentional or not, this often simply arouses emotions about 'outsiders' coming into a country. It is, therefore, necessary to distinguish between different groups and to be clear who exactly we are talking about. This will help us to avoid mixing up categories that should really be distinguished both in our language and in our ethical thinking about the issues.

Refugee

This term is strictly to be applied to those who arrive in a country and are given indefinite leave to remain under the United Nations Convention on the Status of Refugees (1951). This Convention defines a refugee as someone who 'owing to well-founded fear of being persecuted for reasons of race, religion, nationality, membership of a particular social group or political opinion, is outside the country of his nationality and is unable, or owing to such fear, is unwilling to avail himself of the protection of that country; or who, not having a nationality and being outside the country of his former habitual residence as a result of such events, is unable or, owing to such fear, is unwilling to return to it'. In other words, these are people who are forced to leave their home because of the danger of persecution.

Asylum seeker

This category includes all those who, having arrived in a foreign country, apply for refugee status but await a legal judgment as to whether they can legitimately be classed as a refugee. Strictly therefore there cannot be 'bogus asylum seekers' because all those in this group are awaiting a judgment as to whether or not they are genuine refugees in the sense defined above.

Immigrant

In its broadest sense this refers to anyone born outside their country of residence. While it clearly includes refugees and asylum seekers it is a much larger category, and those who arrive as immigrants will do so for a great variety of reasons. Some immigrants have been here for many years (they are often called 'settled immigrants'), whereas others are 'new immigrants' who have recently arrived. In the UK almost half of the immigrant population have become British citizens.

Economic migrant

This term is used for those who move to seek employment and economic benefit in a country other than the one in which they were born. Those granted permission are called *migrant workers*. Some who seek asylum but fail to be granted refugee status may be judged to fall into this category – they are not fleeing persecution but seeking economic advance.

Irregular migrant/illegal immigrant

These are wide-ranging terms that refer to those from abroad who lack legal authorization for their residency in the host country. This would include those whose visas expire and those whose request for asylum is rejected but who then evade authorities and remain in the country, risking arrest and deportation.

Stateless person

This refers to anybody who is not considered a national by any state under its own law. This will include some, but not all, refugees and many who are not refugees.

The common feature of all such groups of people is that they have crossed national state boundaries and moved from one political territory to live within another. A further and increasingly important but often neglected category is that of 'internally displaced persons' (IDPs). These people are defined by the United Nations Office for the Coordination of Humanitarian Affairs as 'persons or groups of persons who have been forced or obliged to flee or to leave their homes or places of habitual residence, in particular as a result of or in order to avoid the effects of armed conflict, situations of generalized violence, violations of human rights or natural or human-made disasters, and who have not crossed an internationally recognized State border'. Although there are estimated to be 3 million IDPs within Europe (twice the number of refugees), they are concentrated in Eastern Europe and the states of the former

Soviet Union and so do not impinge on British life in the same way. This fact is a reminder that we can really only understand the fundamental ethical issues raised by what we think of as 'asylum' and 'immigration' within the UK by looking at the bigger global picture.

The global context and the UK situation

Recent decades have seen a massive rise in the movement of people around the world. In 1960 there were about 75 million people living outside their country of origin but by 2000 this had risen to 175 million. For many these movements across borders are positive, but for millions of men, women and children the departure from their home is a wholly negative experience.

Globally it is internally displaced people who represent the most serious challenge and the most pressing need. Every year since the turn of the millennium there have been about 25 million IDPs, just over half of them within 19 African countries and almost 6 million recently within Sudan alone. Although often spoken of as 'refugees' they do not strictly fall into this category as it is legally defined and so they have to rely on their own governments and international aid agencies for protection and basic human needs.

In addition to IDPs there are those people who are the concern of the Office of the United Nations High Commissioner for Refugees. In 2004 the UNHCR estimated there were 9.2 million refugees (a figure which has been falling since 2000 and is now the lowest in a quarter of a century). The top five hosting countries were Iran (UNHCR estimate: 1,046,000), Pakistan (961,000), Germany (877,000), Tanzania (602,000) and the US (421,000).

In addition to this number of official refugees there were estimated to be over 800,000 people worldwide seeking asylum at the end of 2004. The UNHCR also calculated there to be over 2 million other 'stateless' people. It therefore estimated that the total number of people of concern to them as an organization (including nearly 6 million of the IDPs) was 19.2 million at the start of 2005.

In the context of such massive global movements of people, millions of them displaced involuntarily and facing great need, the facts and figures for the UK perhaps take on a new light:

- About 500,000 people arrive each year to live in the UK for at least a year. Most of these arrive to take up work.
- In summer 2005, the government estimated that about the same number of people (500,000) were immigrants living illegally in the UK.
- Applications for asylum in the UK peaked at just over 80,000 in 2002 but fell back to under 35,000 in 2004.
- In recent years, between 15 and 20 per cent of asylum applicants in any year are granted asylum and become refugees. Around the same proportion are given 'exceptional leave to remain'. However, only about 20 per cent of those refused asylum are believed to have left the country.
- In 2004, for every 1,000 people living in the UK there were 0.7 applications for asylum (roughly the average in the EU).
- In 2004 the main countries of origin of applicants for asylum were: Iran (10.2 per cent), Somalia (7.6 per cent), China (6.9 per cent), Zimbabwe (6.0 per cent), Iraq (5.0 per cent), Pakistan (5.0 per cent), Democratic Republic of Congo (4.3 per cent), India (4.1 per cent), Afghanistan (4.1 per cent) and Sudan (3.8 per cent).

Identifying the issues

Having set the scene and defined some key categories, it is now important to begin to examine some of the key ethical issues that are raised by both the global challenge and by the more specific UK-based concerns in relation to asylum and immigration.

Why do people come to Britain?

To adapt a well-known sound bite, there is little point being tough on asylum seekers unless one is also tough on the causes of asylum seeking. Research into the countries which produce most asylum seekers within Europe suggests there are a number of key factors that explain why people feel they are forced to seek refuge elsewhere. Foremost among these – almost by definition of what is needed to be classed as a refugee – is the treatment of minority groups within the home country, ethnic conflict and abuse of human rights. However, other factors include civil war, the proportion of IDPs to the population, and poverty. Most of those seeking asylum are, it would seem, most probably driven not by the pull of Western wealth but rather by fear and the need to escape from their home country. As a result, responses to the ethical challenges of **war** and **poverty** are highly relevant to issues of asylum and immigration.

Which people get in?

It is now almost universally accepted – even by those whose 'liberal' or 'free market' beliefs might lead them to support free movement of persons as well as goods – that an 'open borders' policy is not a viable policy option. Given the numbers of people on the move across the globe, there needs to be a system of secure boundaries policed by national governments – particularly in the light of fears of international terrorism. It is also still generally accepted that those who are genuine refugees have a right to asylum. Over 142 countries, including the UK, are signatories to the 1951 Refugee Convention and no country has ever withdrawn from the Convention – although some have called for the UK to do so recently. However, between the two boundary-markers of 'not everyone who wants to' and 'all genuine refugees', there are a range of responses which can be divided into those that relate to asylum seekers and those that are applicable to other potential immigrants.

In relation to those seeking asylum, one major ethical question concerns how to reach a judgment fairly and efficiently as to the validity of each individual's claims. Another is how to treat people at various stages of the process: on arrival, when applying, on appeal, after rejection and once recognized as refugees. Government policy is currently under review with new legislation proceeding through parliament.

A variety of ethical concerns have been raised in recent years in relation to treatment of asylum seekers and these need to be weighed in the development of policy. These include:

- the slowness of the processes of assessing claims and the level of legal support and advice provided for those seeking asylum.
- the use of detention powers throughout the process. This is seen by some as 'criminalizing' and as a form of **punishment** afflicted unjustly on weak and vulnerable people, many of whom are fleeing mistreatment. Others, however, argue that it is a necessary measure and may even need to be more widely used for reasons outlined in the next point.
- the ability of asylum seekers to 'slip through the net' and escape the watchful eye of legal authorities. Those who attempt this can then lack social support structures and fall prey to (or become involved in) criminal activity and abuse.

● the level and means of providing financial and welfare support (for example, health care, education for dependants) for those seeking asylum. Currently asylum seekers cannot work for the first year of their application and state support is set at 30 per cent below the normal level of income support.

In these and other areas the tension is that all those who seek asylum are clearly comparatively powerless and poor and in desperate need of the support and care of others. They are also often treated with fear, suspicion and hatred in the media and by sections of society. For Christians, biblical texts such as the Old Testament's concern for the 'alien' and 'sojourner' in the land (Leviticus 19:33–34) and Christ's own teaching about care for the hungry and naked (Matthew 25) are an impetus to do all that is possible to show love to these new and weak neighbours. Many of them are fleeing horrendous persecution and have left behind family, friends and financial support. However, it is also clear that some who claim asylum are not eligible under international agreements and are unjustly and illegitimately seeking to gain entry to the UK and the benefits that come with it. Here, for Christians, the biblical concern that justice must be done and that those in need should receive justice swiftly is a key concern. This not only includes a fair assessment of initial applications but also a just approach in determining such issues as when and how those who have been granted only temporary leave to remain in the country are required to leave and return to their original home.

The issues surrounding immigration are of a different nature. Here it is not so much determining whether or not an individual fits into a defined category (such as 'refugee'), but deciding what levels and which groups of people should be admitted and then how to deal with those who enter and remain in the country illegally. There are clearly many who have concerns about the rise in immigration in recent years. The think tank Migrationwatch UK warns of a net inflow of at least 2 million non-EU citizens per decade and calls for an immigration policy that is 'moderate and managed' because 'massive immigration is contrary to the interests of all sections of our community'.

Despite some of the challenges raised by immigration, there are, of course, often many economic benefits. Countries frequently seek to attract workers from overseas in order to fill gaps within their own labour market due to skill shortages and other causes. The evidence is also that, rather than being a drain economically, migrants contribute more than they take out of the economy. In addition, longer-term demographic changes show that the UK will continue to have many more older people compared to those of working age. This may also encourage us to seek to attract younger, economically active people from abroad.

The current debates revolve around how best to manage and control immigration levels with a recognition that the current system is both too complex and often ineffective. In its place some would prefer the government to set quotas that will limit the number of people allowed to enter each year. Current government proposals, however, favour the development of a single 'points system' in which those seeking to enter and work here are assessed and placed in one of four tiers, depending on their skill levels. Clearly the whole basis of any points system will reflect certain moral values. Ethical questions can be raised here as to whether bringing economic benefit to the UK – which is itself not easy to measure – is given undue prominence at the expense of other goods such as the protection of the needy or the maintenance of family life.

What happens when people are here?

Most of the 'Who gets in?' moral questions are decided procedurally by politicians and bureaucrats although, as we've seen, those procedures have an implicit moral outlook and so can and should be subject to ethical scrutiny. Much more concrete and wide-ranging is the nature of the relationships established between those receiving newcomers and those arriving in a new country. By the very nature of the situation, an 'us'/'them' and 'insider'/'outsider' relationship is established from the start. Personal and political reactions to this raise important ethical questions. One of the most serious moral concerns in recent months and years has been the pattern of response displayed by many areas of the media. Headlines such as 'Kick Out This Scum' and 'Migrant Health Threat to Britain' are not exactly welcoming greetings! Such attitudes and the ways in which they are expressed encourage existing residents to treat their new neighbours with suspicion and fear rather than with generosity and as equals.

Questions are, however, rightly raised as to what entitlements and benefits should accrue automatically to immigrants and, indeed, whether some of those arriving should, perhaps because of the skills they bring, be 'more equal than others'. Clearly a just case can be made that those who have been long-term residents and have contributed socially, economically and through the tax system should be better treated by the welfare state system than those who have just arrived in a country. Nevertheless, to build this strongly into the social system is to institutionalize discrimination, and risks perpetuating inequality and damaging attempts at integration.

The exact nature of the 'integration' expected of immigrants is itself a hotly contested subject. The Conservative politician Norman Tebbitt roused much controversy some years ago when he commented, 'A large proportion of Britain's Asian population fail to pass the cricket test. Which side do they cheer for? It's an interesting test. Are you still harking back to where you came from or where you are?' The selection of British Asians was in part the reason for such a strong reaction to this as it brought a clearly racial element into this test, and thus gave credibility to those who regularly but quite unnecessarily link matters of race and colour to debates about immigration. A cartoon at the time demonstrated the weakness of the 'cricket test' by playing on the old rivalry between Scotland and England and showing a kilted Scotsman claiming he had failed Tebbitt's test.

Integration and social cohesion is clearly of benefit both to those arriving in a new country and to the host society. Neither immigrants nor the population welcoming them should want the creation of separate ghettos or ethnic enclaves. There are, however, real challenges to be faced regarding how far one should go in creating a homogeneous identity – what are the minimum characteristics needed to be an integrated Briton? – and the extent to which greater cultural and social diversity is to be recognized and welcomed. This is especially the case when immigrant populations tend to be concentrated in particular parts of the country: in the UK one-quarter of London's population were born abroad. Furthermore, immigrants are themselves so diverse in their backgrounds and skills that some speak of experiencing 'hyper-diversity', with the latest significant numbers of migrants coming not from the Commonwealth but from Eastern Europe.

Conclusion

The issue of asylum and immigration, although raised in the UK by our own recent domestic experience, needs to be addressed in the light of bigger and stronger global forces. Here it is clear that the ethical challenges discussed in other chapters, particularly those on **war** and **poverty** and to a certain extent on the **environment**, play a significant part in the fact that millions of people around the world are on the move, often against their will and in situations of great need. The questions raised in Britain are simply part of that bigger picture.

There is a deeper ethical challenge underlying the more specific and often technical questions raised in relation to policy details. This is the question of how, as individuals, as communities and ultimately as a nation, we respond to outsiders, especially those who are in most need and who are quite different from us.

The sad fact is that human societies often struggle to welcome fully those who are 'other' and who are obviously different from 'us', whether in skin colour, language, cultural customs or other characteristics. The difficulties this raises are evident from the history of the Christian church. Following the example of Jesus, whom it believes embodies the character of God, the church seeks to welcome the outcast and the stranger. It nevertheless struggled initially to extend beyond Judaism and welcome non-Jews (Gentiles) without expecting them to conform and to become Jews. It has struggled with similar tensions ever since as it has sought through Christian mission to bring new people into its community. On the one hand it expects those who convert to Christianity to share in what the church already is, but it must also be open to them and willing for the church to be changed by them as it welcomes their new cultures and traditions. Similar relational dynamics are in play today in nation states. We are all wrestling with the ethical issues raised by the need to meet the demands of those who arrive at our borders looking for a home, for work or for asylum while simultaneously recognizing the limits and controls that must be put in place without denying people justice.

11. Marriage and Sex

Unlike several of the subjects covered in this book, the focus of this chapter is not some novel ethical issue which we have only been required to think about in the last few decades. Sex is, after all, the concern of 'the oldest profession' and marriage, according to the Bible, goes all the way back to the Garden of Eden. In one sense, then, the moral questions raised are – by definition – as old as the human race. In another sense, however, it is important to realize that our culture's attitudes and practices in relation to sex and marriage have significantly changed in the course of just a few generations. We have experienced what some call a 'sexual revolution'. In addition the twentieth century, particularly since Freud, saw much greater research into human sexuality that has contributed to changing understandings of a number of ethical issues.

Some facts and figures from the UK highlight the changing reality in relation to some of the issues – sex, marriage and cohabitation, and homosexuality – that will be covered in the next few pages.

- In 2005 a UK study of 'lust' as one of the 'Seven Deadly Sins' reported that, whereas in the 1950s 53 per cent of women and 20 per cent of men were married or engaged before having sexual intercourse, by the 1990s this had fallen to fewer than 1 per cent for both men and women.
- The proportion of live births outside marriage quadrupled between 1979 and 1999. By 2003, over 40 per cent of live

births in England and Wales were registered by unmarried couples.

● Until 1967 the male homosexual act – even in private – was a criminal offence but since the end of 2005 same-sex couples can register as civil partners and gain almost all the benefits traditionally linked to marriage.

What's love got to do with it?

Despite these major changes in the pattern of sexual relationships, there remains a considerable consensus that 'good sex' – morally speaking – has to do with love. The most popular reading at weddings probably remains the thirteenth chapter of the apostle Paul's first letter to the Corinthians. Although it says nothing at all about marriage it does give a powerful description of love, particularly what the New Testament in the original Greek calls *agape* love. This is a pattern of love that has shaped Christian moral thinking and, as a result, the understanding of love in all societies influenced by the Christian gospel. *Agape* love is the self-giving love shown to us by God in Jesus. It is the love that always seeks the good of the other who is our neighbour, even if such love is costly to us and even if the one we love appears unlovable or is our enemy. As Paul's 'hymn to love' describes it, 'Love is patient, love is kind. It does not envy, it does not boast, it is not proud. It is not rude, it is not self-seeking, it is not easily angered, it keeps no record of wrongs. Love does not delight in evil but rejoices with the truth. It always protects, always trusts, always hopes, always perseveres. Love never fails' (1 Corinthians 13:4–8).

But of course love has varied forms and manifestations, and if we are to follow Jesus' command and 'Love our neighbour as ourselves', then in one sense love should be universal and not simply related to sex or marriage. There are therefore different kinds of love that have traditionally been distinguished from one another on the basis of four ancient Greek words for various forms of love. *Agape* love is distinguished from how I love my children (referred to in the Greek as *storge* love), which is different from how I love my friends (*philia* love), and that again is not exactly the same as how I love my wife (known as *eros* love or desire).

One of the deeper reasons for the changing pattern of loving sexual relationships in recent years has been the transformation of our understanding and experience of 'love' in a mass, consumerist and market society. It has become what the social thinker Zygmunt Bauman has called 'liquid love'. Love now takes shape in a rapidly moving and changing society that is wary of establishing tight (never mind intentionally permanent) bonds between people. 'Relationships' are therefore formed that are much more loose and contractual arrangements, which are subject to renegotiation and termination. The most intimate of these are usually dependent on 'falling in love' and so often end when we 'fall out of love'. Such 'liquid love' is a quite different phenomenon from the 'solid love' that Paul describes and which has shaped the traditional understanding of marriage.

Marriage – the Judaeo-Christian heritage

Marriage, with some variety in its socially and legally approved forms, is a social phenomenon found across time and space in all human cultures. Western practices have been particularly shaped by the Judaeo-Christian understanding of marriage and sex. This outlook claims that the near-universal practice of marriage in different societies and the common features found in them point to the deeper truth that marriage cannot simply be reduced to a malleable human invention. Nor is 'marriage' something defined simply by the wishes of the individuals involved in the relationship.

Following the example of Jesus as recorded in the gospels, Christians have understood marriage by referring back to 'the beginning of creation' and to the narratives found in the opening chapters of Genesis. In Mark 10:6–8 Jesus, when questioned about marriage, states that 'God made them male and female', citing Genesis 1:27; and in Matthew 19:4–5 he refers back to Genesis 2:24, saying that 'For this reason a man shall leave his father and mother and be joined to his wife and the two shall become one flesh'. On this basis, the Christian understanding is that marriage is part of God's good creation – sometimes called a created institution or a divine mandate. It is therefore much more than a personal choice or a private contract between two people. Marriage from this point of view is ultimately a matter of God's design, with a divinely ordained purpose. It is a unique and exclusive bond between one man and one woman through which they intend to unite themselves together in love throughout their lives in a new structure that is socially distinct from that in which they were born and nurtured.

Stripped of their biblical references and theological rationale, the central features of this vision remain part even of secular marriage law within Britain and in most other traditionally Christian societies. Marriage is a lifelong, exclusive commitment between one man and one woman.

Christians have also seen an even deeper significance in marriage. They have said that it shows us something of the character of God and his relationship of love with us. Within ancient Israel a number of Jewish prophets – most vividly the prophet Hosea – understood there to be a connection between how God made us to relate to one another in marriage and how God himself relates to his people through his self-giving, faithful, persevering covenantal love. In the New Testament, Paul developed this further in his letter to the church in Ephesus in which he understands marriage by reference to the relationship between Christ and the church. This explains why many Christians call marriage (like baptism or holy communion) a sacrament. It also partly explains why issues surrounding sexual ethics and marriage often cause heated controversy within the Christian community.

Despite this high view of marriage, the early Christian church took an even higher view of the way of celibacy in which people renounced all sexual relationships in order to devote themselves fully to the service of God. The danger in emphasizing celibacy was that it could lead to a rejection of marriage as being almost immoral. Faced with this challenge, St Augustine (354–430) – despite his later reputation for being 'anti-sex' – wrote in defence of marriage. In so doing he significantly shaped later Christian understanding through his discussion of 'the goods of marriage'. He identified three such goods: procreation of offspring (*proles*), faithfulness to one's partner (*fides*) and, in relation to Christian marriage, *sacramentum* (by which he meant the permanence of marriage until death that witnessed to God's unfailing love). Although challenged, modified and inevitably misunderstood down through the centuries, the influence of Augustine's approach remains clear. It is still obvious to anyone who attends and listens carefully to any modern Christian wedding service.

The bishops of the Church of England recently explained why marriage is important. Their opening words offer a succinct summary of the significance of marriage and why Christians believe it merits a privileged and honoured place in thinking about love and loving human relationships. Although expressed in Christian terms, many in other faiths (especially Judaism and Islam) and with no religious affiliation would find much that echoes their own vision of love and marriage and their hopes for marriage.

'God is love (1 John 4:16), and in creating human beings he has called us to love, both himself and one another… Marriage is a pattern that God has given in creation, deeply rooted in our social instincts, through which a man and a woman may learn love together over the course of their lives… When publicly and lawfully we enter into marriage, we commit ourselves to live and grow together in this love… Sexual intercourse, as an expression of faithful intimacy, properly belongs within marriage exclusively… Through marriage each of the partners grows in maturity, and is helped to overcome personal failings and inadequacies… By it a new unit of society is created: a couple, stronger than the sum of its members, held together by the bond of domestic friendship. Together the couple can extend love to other people: to their own children, in the first instance, who belong naturally within their domestic circle; and not only to them, but to many others who interact with them in a variety of ways.'
Marriage: A Teaching Document,
House of Bishops of the Church of England

Sex and marriage

The traditional Christian sexual ethic is summarized by the bishops as follows: 'Sexual intercourse, as an expression of faithful intimacy, properly belongs within marriage exclusively.' As the opening facts and figures clearly showed, most people increasingly and openly reject this morality. The restriction it represents is widely seen as unrealistic, repressive of natural desires, and controlling of personal decisions about sexual intimacy. Within the clear moral limits of the participants being consenting adults and with due regard for concerns about health and unwanted pregnancy, whether or not to enjoy the pleasure of sex is generally viewed much more as a matter of personal judgment. Moral decisions are based on the specifics of the couple concerned, especially the nature and expectations of the relationship and the desires of both parties. For some that will result in a fairly 'conservative' attitude about sexual morality, others will adopt a more 'free' attitude to sexual relationships.

To understand the logic of the Christian view that sex should be kept within marriage it is necessary to be clear about the Christian vision of marriage discussed earlier, and also to dig deeper into the Christian view of the meaning and significance of sexual intercourse. This view is what leads to Christian scepticism about claims that sex can mean and signify whatever those engaged in it wish. It also explains why sex is so closely tied to marriage in traditional Christian thinking.

Christians have traditionally viewed sexual intercourse as having both unitive and procreative meaning and significance (for further discussion see **artificial reproductive technologies**). With regard to the relational or unitive good, the significance of sex is summed up by the Bible's vivid physical language of two people 'becoming one flesh'. The apostle Paul even uses this verse from Genesis to describe what happens when Corinthian Christians pop down to the pagan temple for sex with a prostitute (1 Corinthians 6). This 'becoming one flesh' in physical sexual union is intended to represent and to strengthen a deeper emotional and spiritual 'becoming one'. That union, Christians believe, takes place through the making of the lifelong and exclusive commitment of marriage.

In summary, we are both physical and spiritual beings. What we do with our bodies is therefore not detachable from our souls and from who we are as human persons. As a result, there must be a connection between what we say with our bodies and what we say with our life as a whole: as Tom Cruise is told in the film *Vanilla Sky*, 'Don't you know when you sleep with someone… your body makes a promise whether you do or not?' The physical language of total self-giving and bonding that is 'spoken' in sexual intercourse reflects the spiritual language of 'for better, for worse, for richer, for poorer, in sickness and in health… till death us do part' that defines traditional marriage. When 'spoken' in other contexts, therefore, it lies about the meaning of the physical act. It sets the special form of physical lovemaking that uniquely belongs to the distinctive relationship of marriage in the context of a different, less permanent, relationship.

Sexual intercourse is also the means by which new human life arrives in the world. For some this simple 'fact of life' has moral implications that cannot be ignored. Any 'one flesh' union may – even if contraception is used – result in a new human life. That life will need nurture, care, education and love. This means that those who engage in sex must not think only of themselves, either as individuals or as a couple. Because lovemaking is the natural means of baby-making, if the couple are to be morally responsible they must be committed to welcoming and re-ordering their life together in order to serve the needs of any child conceived. If those needs are best met when the child's two parents are genuinely committed to one another as expressed in marriage then it is best for sex to be kept within a marital relationship.

But what of other patterns of sexual relationship? Clearly some of these (for example, sex as a commercial transaction, one-night stands), although they may in some cases be claimed to bring some benefit to someone, are hard to justify morally. Others, however, could be said to approximate to marriage or perhaps even to be treated as in some sense equivalent to marriage, even if they are not formally or legally defined as such. In particular, non-marital cohabitation is now generally accepted in Britain. This new social reality raises a number of ethical questions and deserves some discussion.

Marriage and cohabitation

The figures quoted at the start of this chapter show that setting up home together and starting a family now regularly precede 'tying the knot' by getting married. Over three-quarters of all marriages are now registered with the partners giving the same address at the time of marriage and the majority of church weddings are also of people who are cohabiting. This new social norm means, of course, that just as in the past many young couples who fell in love got married without considering alternative patterns of relationship, so today most will cohabit without viewing their decision as a particularly 'ethical' one or as a rejection of marriage. The practice of cohabitation reflects, to varying degrees in each relationship, the more 'liquid' pattern of loving relationships described by Bauman. But what are the arguments for and against cohabitation as a pattern of sexual relationship?

Arguments for cohabitation

- There are often very practical reasons for cohabitation, in particular, the social and financial costs of developing a loving relationship while living apart and the costs of a wedding (the average cost in the UK is now about £17,500). This can make a period of cohabitation the most efficient use of the limited resources of time and money while developing and strengthening the relationship and thinking about marriage.
- Personal factors are also of vital importance as people make decisions, aware of their own situations and desire for well-being. Many people's experience of marriage – either that of their parents or of their own former marriage – makes it difficult to enter into. Cohabitation then provides an alternative context in which to seek healing and renewed confidence and trust.
- The public, legal and religious elements that are significant in marriage are increasingly considered much less important in our secular 'liquid society' than they were in the past. The fundamental good is to be found in the quality of the relationship (including the sexual relationship) between the two people, and this can be present outside marriage (and can often be lacking within marriage). In contemporary society, cohabitation both expresses that good and provides a context in which it can be nurtured.
- Given the high divorce rate, cohabitation can act as a form of 'trial marriage'. In cohabitation a significant step of commitment is made which may well lead to marriage eventually but from which either party can withdraw without painful legal battles.

Arguments against cohabitation

- There is significant evidence that cohabitation may not be a reliable test for marriage suitability. In 1999 a UK government paper suggested couples cohabiting prior to marriage had a higher risk of marital dissolution than those who did not cohabit. It found that the strongest predictors of divorce were 'age at marriage, premarital childbearing and premarital conceptions, premarital cohabitation and previous marital history'.

- The unreliability of cohabitation as a test for a solid marriage makes sense given that making a formal, exclusive, lifelong commitment in marriage creates a radically different (more 'solid') relationship than that which is present when most people cohabit.

- The social recognition and support provided by legal marriage strengthens the relationship. Although the personal relationship is most important, the wider social and 'institutional' element brought to a relationship by marriage also brings benefits.

- Although marriages can be abusive and oppressive, getting married offers legal protections that are lacking in cohabiting relationships, although this is not always realized by those who believe there is a recognized status of 'common-law spouse'. In contrast, cohabitation involves much greater risk and uncertainty and so lacks the security that may help healing from past hurts.

- Getting married need not be excessively expensive!

These arguments for and against cohabitation risk ignoring another way of looking at the situation. Could cohabiting couples not simply be viewed as married? Many such relationships are lived under the moral disciplines of marriage. They exhibit and encourage exclusive, self-giving love for each other with the intention that this is a lifelong arrangement. A strong case can perhaps therefore be made that the couple's failure to undertake a legal or religious ceremony need not deny their relationship the status of marriage. After all, it was only in 1754, after the Hardwicke Marriage Act, that a ceremony became a legal requirement in England and Wales for the establishing of a marriage.

Although there is much to be said for this line of argument, two challenges remain.

Firstly, to treat cohabitation as equivalent to marriage appears to abandon the importance of explicit, publicly witnessed declarations of lifelong love for enabling a marriage to flourish. Given our society's emphasis on individual preferences and private choices and its reticence (or worse) towards formal public commitments, for many Christians this represents a significant compromise. Nevertheless, the church has always viewed marriage as being established between the two members of the couple and has historically recognized the existence of 'clandestine marriages' that lacked any public ceremony. While never commending this as a way of life – the church was usually critical and looked for formal, public declarations of marriage – such relationships were not always judged to be non-marital.

Secondly, by allowing some cohabiting relationships to be viewed as marriage, this approach easily ignores both the great diversity of relationships that can be described as 'cohabitation' and the difference between marriage and most forms of cohabitation. Judging a certain cohabiting relationship to be genuinely a marriage is something that can only really be done after a long period of time has revealed this to be the truthful reality of the relationship. Many (probably most) cohabitations are not of this form and couples who choose not to marry but rather to cohabit are effectively stating that they do not currently intend to declare and cement their relationship as one of marriage.

Despite such problems with the approach that treats cohabitation as equivalent to marriage, it is interesting to note that Augustine wrestled with some of these questions over 1,500 years ago. He asked at one point whether when two people who are not husband and wife engage in sexual intercourse in faithfulness (even without the desire of children that was so central in his thinking), this is marriage. He concluded that, 'perhaps this may, not without reason, be called marriage, if it shall be the resolution of both parties until the death of one, and if the begetting of children... they shun not'. This is a reminder that what ultimately matters most is the intention of the two people involved and not the marriage ceremony.   As the Christian ethicist Paul Ramsey wrote, 'as difficult as it may be for us to think of a case justifying marriage apart from the ceremony of the legalities, it is important to maintain this as a possibility if only in order to keep clear the meaning of marriage as it has always been understood in the Christian tradition'.

Same-sex marriage?

All the discussion so far has been focused on relationships between a man and a woman, which is the traditional structure of marriage. However, as far as we can tell, most human societies have within them individuals who believe they will find personal fulfilment if their most intimate loving relationship and their sexual behaviour is not within marriage to someone of the opposite sex but in a relationship with someone of the same sex. In many societies openness about this belief and about their sexual attractions is not possible as it risks derision and persecution. In the last forty years, however, in Western society a self-conscious and affirming homosexual identity has developed. Men and women identify themselves as 'gay' and 'lesbian' and seek wider social acceptance and recognition of their loving relationships. Legislative changes in some countries to recognize same-sex marriages or (as in the UK) civil partnerships raise a new set of ethical questions.

Homosexuality: What do we know?

Just how common homosexual attraction is remains unclear and disputed. Although still surprisingly frequently cited, the Kinsey figure of 10 per cent of the population being homosexual is now thoroughly discredited. Different surveys and definitions yield varied results, but in most societies it is probably between 2 and 5 per cent of the population whose sexual attractions are predominantly or exclusively homosexual. Nevertheless, whatever the actual proportions in society, the issue of how to understand and morally evaluate same-sex relationships remains important in our contemporary world.

There also remains great debate as to the causes of homosexuality. Despite occasional media hype about 'gay genes', much of this area remains a great mystery. Broadly speaking some favour a more biological explanation of same-sex attraction (namely that it may be genetic or hormonal or that it may be related to brain size or structure), while others understand it to be more psychological, arising out of patterns of relationships, particularly within the family. What exactly is meant by 'sexual orientation' and whether its cause is nature or nurture or – perhaps most likely – a complex interaction of the two with no standard pattern, will continue to be debated as new evidence comes to light. Whatever conclusions are drawn, the ethical issues remain. This is because they focus on patterns of life for those who, for whatever reason, understand themselves to be homosexual and so look for love with someone of the same sex.

Social and legal changes

In the 1950s people faced arrest and scandal if they were known to engage in homosexual activity. By 2005 many celebrities and public figures are openly gay or lesbian with one newspaper even publishing a 'Pink Power List' of the most powerful homosexual people in the country. That, of course, is not the whole picture. The horrific stories of homophobic assaults and the murders of gay men make clear that many intolerant and morally indefensible reactions to homosexuality remain in our society.

In this context there has been major ethical controversy over whether to lower the age of consent for homosexual acts to equalize it with that for heterosexual activity, and over proposals to recognize and give rights to same-sex partnerships. Recent changes in the law have not gone unchallenged. Particularly among Christians and adherents of the other main monotheistic faiths, there are some who hold the view that such developments are part of a wider moral decline in society rather than evidence of our progress and enlightenment.

Homosexuality: the ethical debate

Underlying the debates over specific changes to legislation have been different ways of approaching the question. For those pressing for changes in the law, the primary motive is often simply the desire for recognition and support for same-sex intimate relationships in order to offer them the prospect of the same quality of life that married couples enjoy. The primary ethical framework used in defence of this position is that of equality and rights. From this perspective, any legal privileging of heterosexuals over homosexuals is discriminatory and fundamentally unfair. Those opposing changes have questioned the nature of sexual orientation and identity (and hence the validity of the hetero/homo distinction). They have also sought to defend the special place of marriage between a man and a woman against what they often see as the immorality of homosexuality.

The arguments in support of some form of 'same-sex marriage' are varied. Central to most is the claim that because some people are inherently homosexually attracted it is unjust for society to privilege marriage between a man and a woman. Although they cannot marry, homosexual people can establish loving relationships that exhibit all the moral qualities found and encouraged within opposite-sex loving relationships such as marriage. Especially given society's historical antipathy towards (and undermining of) such loving same-sex relationships, they now merit greater recognition and support both within society and, some Christians argue, within the church. Just as in heterosexual relationships, stable and committed same-sex relationships need to be encouraged and valued in order to combat transitory or promiscuous patterns of sexual behaviour. Such a pattern of relationship could be called 'same-sex marriage' or – if 'marriage' should be limited to opposite-sex couples – something else. Matters of name are, from this perspective, secondary to the demands of justice. It is this line of argument that underlies the introduction of civil partnerships in the UK at the end of 2005.

In response to these arguments a variety of appeals are made to claim that same-sex relationships should not be viewed as marriage or treated as morally equivalent to marriage. Some of these are based on scripture, others on different sources of authority and wider considerations. Combining both strands, it is argued that 'marriage' has universally been viewed as a contract between people of the opposite sex and that this is in part related to it being a procreative relationship. Marriage understood in this way is part of the foundation of human society and is essential for its preservation and flourishing.

For most Christians the opening chapters of Genesis, which contain the stories of humans being created male and female in the image of God and of Eve being provided by God and hailed by Adam as 'bone of my bone, flesh of my flesh', also give great significance to humanity's division into two sexes. To redefine the structure of 'marriage' to include couples of the same sex is therefore seen as overturning the biblical witness that marriage is a relationship between a man and a woman. It is also to reject a much wider pattern of created order that most societies understand as 'natural'. From this viewpoint, 'same-sex marriage' is not simply a novelty but strictly a self-contradiction. Although this argument is strong in relation to terminology it does not, however, rule out some form of recognition for same-sex relationships that are like marriage but are distinct from it.

The claim that giving formal recognition to same-sex relationships would be wrong often questions the nature and significance of homosexual identity and critiques the claim that some people are inherently homosexually attracted and so their sexual relationships deserve support. Three arguments stand out here.

Firstly, it is claimed that simply recognizing the existence of a phenomenon does not require approval of it. The traditional Christian understanding has been that the experience of homosexual desire is real but that it is one of the consequences of humanity's rejection of God and his will. Until as recently as the early 1970s, homosexuality was also considered a form of psychological disorder open to medical treatment. Some still claim that therapy or forms of Christian healing can help some people experience a re-ordering of their sexual attractions, even to the extent that they are able to function heterosexually. Should such analyses be correct then it would be unwise to give social approval to same-sex relationships.

Secondly, even if, as is likely, such re-orientation proves impossible for many people, there may be many who identify as 'homosexual' but who in fact are capable of marriage. Tom Robinson, writer of the song 'Glad to be Gay' (banned by the BBC in 1977, further evidence that 'The Times They Are A Changin' '), is one famous example. His subsequent marriage helps undermine the simplistic and sharp division of humanity into two fixed sexual orientations. Faced with what is categorized as 'bisexuality' (though adding another label may be unhelpful), some, like Robinson himself, will argue that each person should therefore be totally free to choose whatever form of loving relationship they like and to be supported in that. Others, however, would argue that there are good grounds to prefer marriage and to treat it as normative. Treating marriage on a par with a variety of other loving relationships is seen to undermine marriage and is liable to lead people who would flourish in marriage away from it.

Thirdly, even were it to be granted that some people are inherently homosexual and incapable of finding fulfilment in heterosexual marriage, it does not necessarily follow as a matter of justice or rights that society must reconfigure its moral assessment of loving relationships. To give a parallel example, a case could perhaps be made that some people are inherently 'polyamorous' – they fall in love with and seek sexual relationship with more than one person. The fact that this is the case does not mean that supporting exclusive, lifelong marriage is unjust to such people. Nor would it follow that marriage must instead be defined in a manner that embraces within it polygamy or fixed-term renewable contracts.

Some extend their ethical objections to recognizing same-sex relationships even further and judge them as immoral. A central plank in this argument is that the Bible explicitly condemns homosexual conduct as a form of sexual immorality. Texts in both the Old Testament (the classic story of Sodom in Genesis 19 and two verses of Leviticus in the Old Testament Law) and the New Testament (most fully Paul's words in Romans 1, which include lesbianism as well as male homosexuality) speak strongly against homosexual conduct. There is nothing said positively about homosexual relationships in the Bible; it is always negative. This has been the view of Christians down through the centuries and remains the conviction of the overwhelming majority of Christians as well as Jews and Muslims. They – and others – also sometimes argue that homosexuality is not only 'unbiblical' but 'unnatural'.

A growing number of Christians, however, question whether we can be so certain of God's opposition to homosexuality. Their various arguments fall broadly into two categories. Some argue that the church has simply misread the Bible and has been shaped by cultural prejudices. The texts, it is argued, speak against certain forms of homosexual practice (for example, gang rape in Sodom) but not against loving, permanent, faithful, stable relationships in which love is expressed sexually. Others argue that Christians have never taken all the Bible's commands literally and that we now know much more about human sexuality and can see that some homosexual relationships are good and holy. It is, therefore, acceptable for the church to rethink its traditional position as it has done through the centuries in a number of areas, most recently its attitude to women priests. The traditional argument against homosexual practice, it is claimed, was based on it being unnatural because it was not procreative. However, now we can see homosexuality as 'natural' for some people and, given that we accept contraception and non-procreative heterosexual lovemaking, we cannot any longer object to all homosexual conduct.

Conclusion

The subject of marriage, sex and relationships is one area where much of society now embraces a largely 'privatized' morality in which each person largely does what is right in their own eyes. Compared to many of the other subjects covered in this book there is relatively little public moral debate even though – unlike most other subjects – it is an area in which everyone finds themselves quite regularly having to make moral choices that shape their lives, sometimes in life-changing ways.

Within certain boundaries, most obviously that of not harming others, it is now accepted that the law should not criminalize patterns of sexual behaviour even if people find them distasteful or objectionable. Even sexual conduct that is still generally viewed as immoral such as adultery is the subject of entertainment in TV soaps and celebrity gossip. Moral debates however only usually take place when a senior figure hits the headlines and some claim his 'private morality' (generally a code for 'sex life') renders him unfit for public office.

In contrast to this attitude, the Christian church at times seems almost obsessed with the subject – especially homosexuality – as if it were the only area of ethical significance. While some of that perception is due to the distortion produced by the lens of the media, it is perhaps based on three more serious factors. Firstly, Christians (and those of many other religions) are aware that our most intimate human relationships, what we do with our bodies, and how we express our sexual desires, are not simply a private matter. They are really a sign of the deeper reality of how we as humans understand ourselves and how we understand and relate to God. Secondly, as this chapter has explored, our society's 'traditional' sexual morality was originally strongly shaped by Christian ideas. As this is challenged by new knowledge and by a re-evaluation of previous norms, Christians inevitably struggle with how to respond to a new cultural ethos. Finally, if we are to construct a way of thinking, speaking and acting in relation to marriage, sex and relationships that enables humans to flourish today, it may be that the Christian tradition is what provides us with the necessary categories and tools (even if not all the answers) that are lacking in our 'liquid', individualist, consumerist and often hedonist society.

12. Poverty

It is estimated that on 2 July 2005, 3 billion people watched LIVE 8. Some were undoubtedly only interested in the music and the stars. Most, however, were also drawn to it by what it represented – the demand that the leaders of the most powerful nations of the world represented at the forthcoming G8 Conference (the US, Canada, Great Britain, France, Germany, Italy, Japan and Russia) do something to Make Poverty History. The Make Poverty History campaign, like the Jubilee 2000 campaign before it, has succeeded as a political campaigning group in reaching the parts of the population that traditional political groups cannot reach. It comprises over 400 organizations and has raised awareness of the reality of world poverty, inequality and injustice and of the causes that lie behind these problems.

Making poverty visible

The first challenge that is often faced in relation to popular consciousness about the reality of poverty is that most of us are simply unaware of it in our daily lives. That is true within our own nation and even within our own neighbourhoods. Like the poor man, Lazarus, in the parable Jesus told (recorded in the gospels in Luke 16), those of us who are (at least relatively) rich and wealthy often seem able simply to ignore the existence of poverty – even the most extreme poverty, even when it is on our doorstep. This is not just true domestically. It is also often true internationally, despite media coverage and shocking images of starving children. The facts are stark but, until recently, are rarely publicized:

● Half the world's population lives on less than $2 a day. In sub-Saharan Africa there are over 300 million people living on less than $1 a day.

● Many of the poorest countries spend more on debt repayment than on health or education.

● Over 1 billion people worldwide lack reliable access to safe drinking water.

● Some 10.6 million children under five die every year. More than 4 million of these are in Asia and the Pacific.

● In Africa more than 44 million primary-school-aged children are out of school.

● The UN estimates that 7 million children die unnecessarily each year. The main causes are curable diseases and unclean water that could be made safe.

● This year a million or more Africans will die of malaria and 2 million will die of AIDS.

● Around 30,000 people die every day because of poverty.

What's wrong?

Faced with such data we find – in contrast with almost all the other ethical issues discussed in this book – universal agreement. It is accepted that such a situation is not good and so things needs to be changed. Many would even go as far as to call the current situation 'evil'. Poverty is not good because it is destructive of human well-being. It deprives people of the ability to grow and fulfil their potential, and ultimately it kills, not just spiritually but physically.

From a Christian perspective, such extreme poverty is intolerable. The 'ethical issue' most frequently raised by Israel's prophets when they challenged God's people is that of economic injustice and this theme is also central in Jesus' message which he proclaimed as 'good news to the poor'. Since the Exodus of the Hebrew slaves from Egypt, God has consistently shown himself to have what has been called 'a bias to the poor'. The existence of poverty is a denial of the intrinsic and equal value of every single human being as someone made in the image of God. It also denies God's purposes for the human race in giving us so many material goods in creation. As the Roman Catholic Second Vatican Council declared, 'God intended the earth and all it contains for the use of everyone and of all peoples; so that the good things of creation should be available equally to all.'

The language of 'equally' highlights an issue that is related to, but which must also be kept distinct from, that of poverty. What makes the levels of world poverty especially shocking and scandalous is the contrast that exists between the standard of living and quality of life of the world's poor and that of probably all those reading this book. For some people, any and all economic inequalities are to be understood as a sign of injustice and so must be eradicated. Most people, though, recognize that an absolute equality in all goods is neither achievable nor desirable. However, when there is gross inequality in the provision of such basic human goods as education and health and when the economic gap between rich and poor is so vast that the poorest are literally being left to die because of their poverty, then moral justification of such inequality becomes impossible.

Alongside agreement that there is a real and deep problem there is also a growing consensus as to which injustices lead to these problems. One major ethical challenge facing many of the poorest nations is undoubtedly corruption in systems of government and in social and economic structures. This may be combined with the tyranny of dictatorship. Domestic politicians in some poorer nations can also be criticized for their allocation of resources, such as the 2003 Kenyan parliament decision approving $10 million for new cars for each of its 223 MPs. While the gap between rich and poor nations is shocking, there is also great inequality within the poorer nations with the powerful amassing great wealth without regard for the poor. Clearly serious moral questions can be raised about the internal politics and economics of many poor nations. However, to focus on this is to forget that the wealthy and powerful in rich countries also often benefit themselves at the expense of their own domestic poor. This can also imply that the fundamental problems are internal to poor societies. The reality, it is becoming widely recognized, is that the root causes are international and relate to our global economic systems. In particular, the patterns of international trade and lending on interest are a major structural force for injustice and poverty.

Ethical economics?

One of the paradoxes in our contemporary situation is that although there is widespread disgust at the destructive power of poverty, there is also still a strong sense that economics is a 'science'. As such it is thought that it must therefore be kept almost wholly separate from issues of ethics and morality and maintain some form of 'objectivity'. Of course, in practice there are certain laws that have a moral basis and which govern even 'free markets'. These, for example, seek to prevent the use of violence or fraud in economic exchanges. As we have seen, it is the failure of certain poorer countries to adhere to these that leads to corruption flourishing, and this in turn is one factor in creating poverty. The deeper problem, however, is the refusal to think ethically about economic theory and practice. Such thinking would, inevitably, raise questions about the rationale behind what is variously called 'liberal free-market economics' or 'global capitalism'. It would also challenge the imbalance of power within the world economy that perpetuates much injustice.

The underlying framework of the economic theory that shapes our current international economic system is one that places the freedom and rights of the individual at the heart of economic exchanges. In particular, there are property rights that allow those who possess goods to control them and to trade them in the market place in order to benefit themselves and maximize profits. Following the vision of Adam Smith, it is reckoned that such a free market mechanism will, by the 'invisible hand' of market forces, bring economic benefit to all through such self-seeking competitiveness. The problem is that the stark reality of world poverty invalidates this theory and discredits economic structures that are built upon it.

Faced with the failure of both economic theory and practice, older approaches to economics that understood our commercial transactions within a much broader ethical framework may need to be revived and applied to contemporary challenges. Within such historical economic thinking, much of which was shaped by the Judaeo-Christian outlook on the world, the way that material goods were viewed and shared between people was a central *ethical* issue. Private property and wealth were accepted – in contrast to some later Marxist and anarchist economic thinking

– but they were viewed much more in terms of a trust to be used for the benefit of the community as a whole. They were not something to be accumulated for private benefit. Nor were possessions to be left solely at the disposal of their individual owner who was subject to no moral constraints or accountability. Furthermore, when it came to the exchange of goods there was such a thing as a 'just price'. This was not simply determined by the power play of market forces. Such 'free market' forces, unless placed in – and limited by – a wider vision of human flourishing, make the poorest into the weakest in the determination of market prices. The poor are therefore placed at the mercy of those whose economic power enables them to dominate and to act unjustly.

Fair trade?

One major reason for continuing poverty in many parts of the world is that the goods that are produced by the people of that country are unable to provide them with sufficient money to invest for their future in health and education. In some cases they do not receive enough even to survive. There are a number of different economic structures and practices that contribute to this situation. This leads many to conclude that the fundamental problem is not with the producers in poorer nations and the quality of their goods but rather with an international economic system that is simply not fair. The effect of changes to the trading system is difficult to measure but it could be enormous. The following four aspects of economic life are major contributors to world poverty. Despite the claim of some that economics should be left to business, profits and free markets, they raise major ethical challenges.

Subsidies and dumping of goods

It is common in most countries for governments to subsidize certain products. However, when wealthy countries do this for one part of their relatively strong economies, the effect can be devastating on poorer countries for which that product is vital to their trading power. Rich countries spend $1 billion every day on agricultural subsidies. They then often 'dump' the surplus they cannot sell in home markets on the world market (for example, the EU dumps 5 million tonnes of surplus sugar on the world market). This often has devastating effects for poorer nations.

A classic example is the American cotton industry. The US spends more on cotton subsidies than any other country – about $4.5 billion in subsidies each year. America's 25,000 cotton farmers therefore get a subsidy of $230 per acre, a total amounting to more than three times the entire US aid budget for Africa's 500 million people. As a result, America exports 75 per cent of their harvest and controls 40 per cent of world trade. This has been a major factor in world cotton prices falling by 30 per cent between 2004 and 2005. The effect on countries such as Mali and other cotton-producing countries in Africa – which often produce cotton at a lower cost – is enormous. For example, it is reckoned that since 2001, the four West and Central African cotton producers (Benin, Burkina Faso, Chad, and Mali) – in which over 10 million people depend on cotton production – have suffered export losses of around $382 million because of US subsidies.

Trade barriers

In addition to subsidizing goods for export, many richer nations limit access to their markets by their tax regimes. These place heavy tax burdens on poorer countries that are trying to export into wealthy nations. One effect is that the wealthier nations import raw materials (such as cocoa) that they then turn into finished products (such as chocolate) that they can sell on the world market at great profit. Poorer nations seeking to mirror this practice and to protect themselves from imports run the risk of losing aid and loans if their barriers harm the wealthier nations. Import barriers are up to four times as high for poorer nations trying to sell in the world market than they are for wealthy nations. It is calculated that trade restrictions in rich countries cost developing countries around $100 billion a year, which is twice as much as they receive in aid. Particularly hard hit are sub-Saharan Africa ($2 billion) and India and China (over $3 billion).

The effect of changes here could be enormous. If poor countries' share of world exports could be raised by just 1 per cent, the money generated might enable as many as 128 million people to be lifted out of poverty. In Africa, for example, a 1 per cent rise in share of exports would generate $70 billion which amounts to more than five times what the continent receives in aid.

Working conditions

In addition to the hurdles faced when goods come to market, inequality is also found much earlier in the process. Wealthy multinational companies can set very low standards of working conditions and remuneration for workers in poor countries in a way they are less able to do at home. This is particularly evident in food and clothing industries and women are especially hit by such practices. Oxfam's study 'Trading Away Our Rights' has, for example, discovered that among Chile's women fruit-pickers no less than 75 per cent are now on temporary contracts. They work

60 hours per week in season and yet a third of them are still earning below the minimum wage. In Bangladeshi garment factories less than half the women working have a contract and most get no maternity or health coverage.

Primary commodity prices

Many of the poorest countries of the world rely economically on primary commodities – a product in a raw or unprocessed state such as coffee, cotton or copper. It is estimated that more than 50 developing countries depend on three or fewer such commodities for more than half of their export earnings. The problem is that prices for these goods on the world market are often low and highly unstable. The classic case is that of coffee. There have been massive drops in its price in recent years. For example, between 1999 and 2000, the price of coffee fell by 50 per cent to a 30-year low so that the 'real' price of coffee was just 25 per cent of its level in 1960. This has had a devastating impact on 25 million coffee producers around the world while large companies have continued to make significant profits.

In response to these challenges there have been two levels of ethical response that seek to redress the imbalances and work for a more just trading situation that will in turn help to alleviate world poverty.

Political pressure on international economic organizations

As evidenced in the run-up to the Edinburgh G8 Conference in 2005, there is growing popular unhappiness with the current situation. Pressure is increasing on governments in the wealthy nations to work through organizations such as the World Trade Organization to reform the current international trading system. Organizations such as Oxfam and the wider Make Poverty History coalition continually challenge governments to think beyond their own national and regional self-interest in trade negotiations and to act instead for justice and for the world's poor. Such measures are, however, slow and many governments are wary of agreeing to changes that could harm domestic producers and consumers and so make them unpopular at home.

Growth of Fairtrade products

Alongside the large-scale government pressure there is the development of alternative trading patterns that are sensitive to ethical issues such as the need for a just price and good working conditions. One of the great success stories here is in relation to coffee (where Fairtrade products are increasing their market share), but increasingly there is a much wider range of fairly-traded products readily available to shoppers. In the UK the Fairtrade Foundation was formed in 1992 and has clear standards for a range of commodities. Retail sales of Fairtrade products are increasing by over 40 per cent each year as consumers readjust their shopping patterns in order to support structures that are not complicit in the more ethically dubious practices of world markets. These developments remind us that even shopping is a major ethical issue and that, although they are very small-scale, each of us makes decisions that can either support the current system or encourage more just alternatives.

Drop the debt?

Alongside the structure of the world's trading system, the world's financial systems have also been subject to much ethical scrutiny in the last decade. It has become increasingly obvious that the lending policies of both banks and governments in the rich developed world have played a part in perpetuating and increasing levels of poverty in African countries and in other parts of the globe. Through the 1960s and 1970s the world's poorest countries were encouraged to borrow from developed countries and international financial institutions. The result is that at present low-income countries owe rich countries over $500 billion and give back over $100 million each day in the servicing of their debts.

As a result of falls in commodity prices, the rise in oil prices and increased interest rates, the international debt crisis began to come to a head and gain public attention in the late 1980s. The total debt owed by developing countries more than doubled between 1980 and 1990. It was clear that loans to some countries had been misused and had not benefited the people of those countries through wise investment. Often, though, those lending should have been aware of this reality as billions of dollars of debt arises from loans made to dictators. More seriously, it was clear that the level of debt many countries now faced was totally unsustainable – particularly given the interest being demanded on loans. Poor countries were caught in a trap: although they were receiving aid from developed countries, in order to service their debt they were paying back more than they received in aid. So, between 1970 and 2002, the poorest African countries received $294 billion in loans but they paid back $298 billion in interest payments and repayments of principal. This still left them owing more than $200 billion to their wealthy creditors. Nigeria, for example, has borrowed $17 billion and repaid $18 billion yet it still owes $34 billion. The current situation is that for every dollar received in grant aid, low-income countries pay back $3. In short, the rich are getting richer and the very poor are getting even poorer as a result of the debt crisis.

By 1996, the key financial institutions – the World Bank and the International Monetary Fund (IMF) – were launching a scheme to reduce the debt of 'Heavily Indebted Poor Countries' (HIPCs). This scheme sought to view the situation as a whole rather than dealing with individual debts separately and it included debts to the World Bank and IMF.

In 1997 a campaign was formed that, remarkably, took its name and inspiration from a rather obscure piece of Jewish law in one of the least read Old Testament books. This was the 'Jubilee legislation' found in Leviticus 25:8–12. That legislation sought to prevent accumulation of land within ancient Israel by requiring that it be returned to its owners every fifty years. The campaign drew on this vision of economic justice and also picked up a statement by Pope John Paul II. In 1994 he looked forward to the millennium and said, 'Thus in the spirit of the book of Leviticus, Christians will have to raise their voice on behalf of the poor of the world, proposing the Jubilee as an appropriate time to give thought, among other things, to reducing substantially, if not cancelling outright, the international debt which seriously threatens the future of many nations.'

Inspired by such a vision, the Jubilee 2000 campaign was formed, drawing together people of all faiths and of none from across the world. In May 1998, in a precursor to Edinburgh 2005, a human chain 9 km long was formed by over 70,000 people in Birmingham – where the G7 (as it was then) was meeting – calling for a cancellation of debt. By the millennium, nearly 25 million people from 166 countries had signed a petition stating that 'the start of the new millennium should be a time to give hope to the impoverished people of the world' and so affirming that 'to make a fresh start, we believe it right to put behind us the mistakes made by both lenders and borrowers, and to cancel the backlog of unpayable debts of the most impoverished nations'. Although these demands were not met, the campaign successfully raised public awareness and led to new measures being taken that, though less than desired, have given some assistance.

The current system is still focused on what the World Bank and IMF class as HIPCs. To be considered an HIPC eligible for debt relief, a country must meet two main criteria. They must:

- face an 'unsustainable debt burden, beyond available debt-relief mechanisms';
- establish a track record of reform and sound policies through IMF and World Bank supported programmes.

While obviously intended to prevent abuse of the debt-relief system, these criteria make it more difficult for some poor and needy countries to qualify. They can also impose on those seeking relief a set of economic policies in terms of liberalization and privatization. Many believe that these measures may not be beneficial and that it is wrong for them to be determined and imposed by undemocratic organizations that are dominated by representatives of the wealthy developed world.

A total of 42 countries have qualified for debt relief as HIPCs and are at various stages in the programme. Following the Edinburgh G8 meeting it has been agreed that 18 of these countries should receive 100 per cent cancellation of outstanding debts to the World Bank, IMF and African Development Fund. Although the agreement to 100 per cent cancellation marks a significant precedent, this development still leaves major challenges for many other countries. Debt-relief campaigners claim that no less than 60 countries need 100 per cent debt cancellation if they are to be able to meet the Millennium Development Goals discussed below.

The Old Testament contains many condemnations of taking interest on a loan, particularly from those who are poor and in need. Jesus famously urged his disciples to give without expecting to receive back. As a result, for many centuries the Christian church opposed the taking of interest. This practice is still condemned within Islam. Debt cancellation, like all forms of amnesty and forgiveness, can appear to be unjust and to reward those who have been negligent or even corrupt in their financial commitments. Nevertheless, if there is to be any chance of 'making poverty history' then further and more generous programmes of debt relief appear to be essential.

Millennium development goals

Faced with the various challenges of world poverty, in September 2000 all 191 member states of the United Nations pledged themselves to meet eight goals by 2015. These are:

1. **Eradicate extreme poverty and hunger.**
2. **Achieve universal primary education.**
3. **Promote gender equality and empower women.**
4. **Reduce child mortality.**
5. **Improve maternal health.**
6. **Combat HIV/AIDS, malaria and other diseases.**
7. **Ensure environmental sustainability.**
8. **Develop a global partnership for development.**

Within each of these goals, specific targets have been set. So, for example, in relation to poverty the plan is to reduce by half (between 1990 and 2015) the proportion of people living on less than a dollar a day and to reduce by half the proportion of people who suffer from hunger. While significant progress is being made in some areas and in relation to some goals, it is already being admitted that in many parts of the world – most notably sub-Saharan Africa – these goals show no signs of being reached by the target date. In early 2005, the Chancellor of the Exchequer, Gordon Brown, admitted that on present progress the first target would not be met in sub-Saharan Africa until 2130. It is therefore clear that in relation to trade policy, debt relief and other policies – not least the level and structure of international aid – the ethical challenges of world poverty will remain.

Conclusion

Unless you are a fast reader, in the time it has taken you to read this chapter, over 200 people in the world will have died from starvation, most of them children under five. A few dozen African children will also have died of malaria. Of all the ethical issues discussed in this book, that of poverty is perhaps the most pressing. It is also the most scandalous given the wealth and technological power to be found in our world. Poverty does not of course stand alone and unrelated to other issues. The challenges raised in relation to the **environment** and particularly to war join the economic factors discussed here in contributing to the injustices that produce such human suffering.

The myth is that we can solve the problem of poverty without bearing any of the cost ourselves. That myth is why reform to trade rules and debt-relief programs has so far been so comparatively minor and has proved to be relatively ineffective. The reality is, however, that our relative wealth and prosperity is not unconnected to the absolute poverty of many others with whom we share this planet. In the words of the early Christian theologian Ambrose, 'It is the hungry man's bread that you withhold, the naked man's cloak that you store away, the money that you bury in the earth that is the price of the poor man's ransom and freedom.' In such situations the reality is that poverty can only really be made history if the rich make some sacrifices. The words of that great Jewish prophet Jeremiah stand over 2,000 years later as a stark warning from the God of the poor: 'Woe to him who builds his house by unrighteousness, and his upper rooms by injustice; who makes his neighbours work for nothing, and does not give them their wages.' (Jeremiah 22:13).

13. Euthanasia

'It's not that I'm afraid to die, I just don't want to be there when it happens,' quipped Woody Allen. But just as we have no say in or control over our beginnings, so we generally have little or no say in or control over our endings. Death visits us. And yet we increasingly seek to be able to give ourselves a 'good death' (the literal translation of euthanasia) by, paradoxically, 'being there when it happens' because we make it happen.

'Euthanasia' has come to mean the deliberate decision to kill a human being not out of anger or as an act of execution for wrongdoing but because their life is considered to be not worth living. In the words of Pope John Paul II, 'Euthanasia here means an action or omission that by its nature or by intention causes death with the purpose of putting an end to all suffering. Euthanasia is, therefore, a matter of intention and method.'

In this chapter, after a quick survey of what is meant by 'death', we will look at the different types of euthanasia and what it means to be a person. The central areas of dispute will then be examined by looking at the difference between killing someone and letting them die, the principle of double effect, whether one has a right to die and some of the ethical questions and concerns that would be raised were euthanasia to become an acceptable practice.

When does death occur?

' 'E's passed on! This parrot is no more! He has ceased to be! 'E's expired and gone to meet 'is maker! 'E's a stiff! Bereft of life, 'e rests in peace! If you hadn't nailed 'im to the perch 'e'd be pushing up the daisies! 'Is metabolic processes are now 'istory! 'E's off the twig! 'E's kicked the bucket, 'e's shuffled off 'is mortal coil, run down the curtain and joined the bleedin' choir invisible!! THIS IS AN EX-PARROT!!'

John Cleese's famous outburst in *Monty Python* raises the question of when, strictly speaking, we become an ex-human. And here, as with questions about the start of life (see the chapter on **embryos**), any judgment has to take seriously the biological evidence and medical opinion. Ancient religious texts give little concrete assistance and, in the middle of the twentieth century, Pope Pius XII made it clear that 'The task of determining the exact instant of death is that of the physician.' That instant is not, in fact, quite as obvious as we might think, particularly given our growing knowledge and changing technology.

Perhaps the simplest and most obvious answer would be to say that someone is dead when they stop breathing. That was the standard understanding until the seventeenth century. Then in 1628 it was discovered that the heart pumped blood, and the key criterion became probably the other standard popular answer you'd get from a non-expert: death happens when the heart stops. That served well until, in the 1960s, doctors began to perform operations such as bypass surgery during which the heart of the patient is stopped. It then became possible to resuscitate someone, rush them to hospital and put them on a respirator that breathed for them, even if the damage to their brain was so great that they had no chance of long-term survival if it was turned off. It seems that the owner of the parrot shop could have a case – it is not always as easy as we might initially think to tell whether something is dead!

The modern, generally accepted medical definition of death is that death happens when someone is 'brain dead'. Back in 1968 the Harvard Committee recommended that cessation of brain activity replace cessation of heart and lung activity as the formal definition of death. It is important to realize that this refers to whole brain death and not just the death of higher brain function. One of the challenges is that it is therefore possible for a 'dead person' to have 'live organs', especially as we have the technology to separate out different bodily functions and keep them going artificially. Someone may therefore be brain dead but continue to breathe by means of a machine, perhaps in order to enable organ transplantation.

Persistent vegetative state

Although it is a very rare condition, in both the UK and the US the circumstances surrounding patients who are in a persistent vegetative state (PVS) have led to questions about euthanasia hitting the headlines. In 2005, the case of Terri Schiavo dominated the news. After fifteen years in PVS, her husband – whose motives were widely questioned – sought, successfully, to bring her life to an end against the wishes of her parents and other family members. The method used to end her life was the same as had been used over ten years earlier in another famous case, this time in the UK. In this instance the life of Tony Bland, a young victim of PVS following the 1989 Hillsborough disaster, was brought to an end by the removal of his food and water supply – although in his case both family and doctors were fully supportive of the request.

Both these cases were seen as watershed decisions. This is because PVS patients are clearly alive and they would continue to live without any major invasive intervention even though damage to their brain cortex means their capacity for any meaningful human interaction is minimal or non-existent. The decision to withhold treatment was therefore clearly a decision to bring their lives to an end.

An ex-person?

A common defence of such action is that patients who have been in PVS for some time are, though alive, no longer human persons. They – and some patients suffering from other conditions – lack the basic qualities we associate with being human. These qualities include interaction with other humans, consciousness, ability to feel joy and pain, and preferences for their life and its future direction. As such they are no longer judged to be human persons (just as, from this perspective, the **embryo** is considered not to be a fully human person in the early stages of life). So, Terri Schiavo's husband placed on her tombstone the claim that she 'departed this earth' on the day she entered PVS but was only 'at peace' when she died. If some people are to be seen as 'ex-persons' then perhaps we are free to treat them differently in terms of how we respect their life. Indeed, some would argue we *should* treat them differently, just as we treat **animals** differently.

Most Christians have objected strongly to these ideas, as developed by ethicists such as Peter Singer and John Harris. They have emphasized that as creatures of the creator God, all living human beings – even, perhaps especially, the weakest, most vulnerable and most dependent – are made in the image of God. We must therefore not create a sub-category of 'human persons' that devalues those lives that fall outside this group, and considers them to be 'ex-persons' whom it is permissible to kill. There is also concern that cases such as that of Tony Bland lead to a downward trend, with more and more people being placed in this group and being treated as if their lives are somehow of less worth. This in turn makes others fearful that they might end up being classed in this category. In the UK, the original and very limited decision to permit withdrawal of food and water from Tony Bland and PVS patients has expanded in its scope. This has led Lee Burke, who suffers from a degenerative brain condition, to seek legal assurances in the courts that he will not have food and water withheld from him if he becomes unconscious.

Some Christians, however, have been concerned that the definition of what it means to be human should not be reduced to a solely biological understanding of what it means to be alive. They have stressed that the call to be God's image means there may be 'biological life' in that the person is biologically alive, but no 'biographical life' because the person is wholly incapable of ever again being a conscious interactive human subject. Where there is no ability to recognize and respond to God's call and so no ability to live a responsible biographical life, there may not be the same 'sanctity of human life' to be respected.

Types of euthanasia

The examples of Tony Bland and Terri Schiavo illustrate that there are different forms of euthanasia depending on the role the patient plays in the decision-making. In these cases, the patient is clearly incapable of giving any input to the decision because of their medical condition. In other situations, however, the patient is much more involved. So, in another famous case, the UK courts decided in 2001 that Dianne Pretty's husband could not be given permission to help her end her own life. She wished to do this because of the degenerative effects produced by motor neurone disease.

The following distinctions are often therefore drawn when discussing euthanasia.

Involuntary euthanasia
Here the person does not wish to have their life ended but their wishes are ignored. The classic example is the Nazi euthanasia programme imposed on people judged worthless by the regime.

Non-voluntary euthanasia
Here the person is unable to express their wishes but their life is ended (as in the cases of Tony Bland and Terri Schiavo).

Voluntary euthanasia
Here the person clearly expresses a desire for their life to be ended (as in the case of Dianne Pretty), or consents to be killed.

The Dianne Pretty case illustrates another form of killing often classified as 'euthanasia'. Strictly speaking, her husband would not have killed her but would have helped her to commit suicide (self-killing). Such forms of euthanasia are 'assisted suicide' and, where specialist knowledge is required, this might be 'physician assisted suicide' (PAS). Unlike suicide both of these are currently illegal in the UK.

Active and passive euthanasia?

Sometimes a distinction is made between active and passive euthanasia. In 'active euthanasia', direct action is taken to bring about the person's death. A famous example is that of Lillian Boyes, who suffered from chronic rheumatoid arthritis and had often expressed a wish to die. In August 1991 her family doctor, Dr Nigel Cox, eventually injected her with a large and lethal dose of potassium chloride and she quickly suffered a heart attack that killed her. In 'passive euthanasia', a decision is made not to follow a particular course of action in order to bring about the person's death. The withdrawal of food and water shows the difficulty of dividing these two categories. Is this active, in that one removes feeding tubes, or is it passive, in that one simply refrains from providing something essential for life that is now classed as 'medical treatment'?

The distinction is not only difficult to apply in many cases; it is also unhelpful ethically. What is held in common – the intention to bring about another's death, whether by action or inaction – is the morally significant factor. By forgetting this key fact passive euthanasia is sometimes made the same as 'letting die', but these two are not morally equivalent.

Killing and letting die

The focus on intention to kill is a central but contentious aspect of debates about euthanasia and what ultimately distinguishes even 'passive euthanasia' from 'letting die'. It has always been recognized that patients have a right to refuse treatments and that it is possible to do so without being guilty of intentionally seeking death. The treatment may be considered excessively burdensome or of little benefit and the patient is not morally obliged to do all in their power to stay alive. One obvious and common example is the decision to turn off life-support systems. The intention here is presumably not to kill – were the person to remain alive, the decision would not be judged a failure – even though in almost all cases death is the foreseen result.

More difficult is when the decision not to intervene is made by someone else on behalf of a patient, especially when the patient is a child. In 2004 and 2005, the parents of seriously ill one-year-old Charlotte Wyatt unsuccessfully sought to require doctors to resuscitate her if she again stopped breathing. Here it was not a case of intentionally killing the baby by 'passive euthanasia' but rather of letting her die. While the decision to 'let die' by refusing or withdrawing some treatment may in some situations amount to 'killing by omission' – for example, many would say this is clearly the case when food and water is withdrawn – it need not always be seen as a form of euthanasia.

Double effect

The other complex area that needs to be noted before examining arguments for and against euthanasia is what is called 'double effect' (see also the discussion on discrimination in the chapter on war). Those who argue for greater acceptance of euthanasia sometimes claim it is already accepted in palliative care, where drugs are given that kill patients. Here again the question of intention is vitally important.

As anyone who reads leaflets from the pharmacy knows, all drugs have 'side-effects'. In taking them, however, we do not seek to produce these side-effects. We seek the primary effect: healing the ailment they claim to cure. Similarly, those who administer pain-killing drugs do not intend to kill their patients by doing this. If they did then they would do better to follow Dr Cox and use potassium chloride or some other lethal drug. They intend to ease pain and this is a good and honourable intention. It may be that a side-effect or 'double effect' of this action is that the patient's life is shortened, but that is not what is sought. Here it is crucial to distinguish between aim and intention on the one hand and consequence or result on the other. The consequence of a particular procedure may be the same as for another procedure but that does not mean the two acts are morally equivalent. One procedure may intend and seek the consequence; another may foresee it but not seek to bring it about.

The right to die?

As with many other moral debates today, at the heart of the claims made by those arguing for acceptance of euthanasia lies the language of rights. We have, it is claimed, the 'right to die'. It is, however, important to be clear that this 'right' is quite different from any other right we claim. Firstly, if exercised, it eliminates the person who claims those other rights. Secondly, it is also a claimed right to be able to destroy something, in this case one's own life. Expressed in these terms, the obvious question that must be raised is whether or not one has such an absolute right over what one claims to be able to destroy.

Two related objections can be made to the 'right to die'. Firstly, it is difficult, perhaps impossible, to justifiably claim such a total and absolute right over one's own life. My life is a life shared with others. Most directly my life is part of the life of my family and closest friends. They can therefore be said to have an interest in what I am claiming a right to destroy. Their lives will be affected if I exercise my 'right to die'. The experience of suicide shows how negative and destructive the taking of a life can be on those closest to the person who dies. In short, my life is not just my own and so my claim to be able to extinguish it – my 'right to die' – cannot be accepted without question or qualification.

Secondly, Christians and other theists wish to press this insight further by speaking of life as a gift from God. Our life is therefore certainly not ours in such a way that we can bring it to an end whenever we desire and will to do so. Indeed, the consistent witness of the Christian church has been that to directly and intentionally bring about the death of an innocent human person is always wrong. It represents a grasping and extinguishing of something that should instead be received with thanks, trusting that it is and remains God's good gift to us.

But, of course, just as some gifts we get at Christmas are not really wanted, so our lives may become so limited or filled with pain that we don't really want this gift. This is where the advocates of euthanasia combine their appeal to rights with their protest against suffering to present a strong case that euthanasia must be permitted.

Who decides and how?

The challenge, of course, is to clarify who decides when a life is 'not worth living' and on what basis one could legitimately exercise a 'right to die'. Almost all emphasize that euthanasia should be voluntary and all oppose the projects of state euthanasia developed in Germany under the Nazis. However, the cases of Tony Bland and Terri Schiavo remind us that some of the most heart-rending cases do not involve voluntary choice for death by the patient. This also highlights that indeed 'no man is an island', and that decisions we make for ourselves help shape the social context and expectations in which decisions are made by and on behalf of others.

Behind support for voluntary euthanasia there is a strong emphasis on patient autonomy – the individual's right to choose. But this gives no basis on which to determine whether or not something is a good choice. If I have a 'right to die', can I exercise that at any time I wish or do I need to meet certain criteria? Few would support there being no constraints. After all, when faced with someone who is suicidal we usually try to persuade them not to kill themselves. But in that case how do we determine those constraints and how tight should they be?

As soon as we say that some requests for euthanasia should not be supported (even if sincerely and freely made by the patient) but some requests should be accepted, we do two things. Firstly, we admit that there is not a universal human 'right to die' in the way we would claim, say, a 'right to food and water' – only those who meet certain conditions are able to claim this right. There are, in other words, limits placed on any individual's freedom to choose to die. Secondly, we grant that there are some situations in which it is reasonable and acceptable to reject life and to seek to be killed. One of the concerns of those opposed to euthanasia is that this easily slips into it becoming unreasonable and socially unacceptable for people in such situations to continue to accept life and to refuse to be killed. This is especially the case when staying alive means they will continue to drain limited resources in health care. If it is reasonable for people suffering from a certain disease or reaching a certain age to seek to end their life and if more and more people in those situations do so, then the pressure builds on anyone who falls ill with that disease or passes that age barrier to do everyone the service of volunteering for euthanasia. They are, after all, living a life that society has judged to be – in at least some cases – not really worth living. It is, therefore, difficult to say to them without qualification, 'It is good that you are alive.'

Protection of the weak and vulnerable

One of the main arguments, therefore, against accepting euthanasia is that having strict laws and social norms opposed to it is an important and necessary way of protecting the weak and vulnerable. Almost by definition, those who make a request for their life to be ended are weak and not satisfied with life, even when they display the strength and vigour demonstrated by Dianne Pretty when arguing for her 'rights'. The concern is that if euthanasia were permitted, this would place further pressure on those who perhaps already feel they are an excessive and unjustifiable burden on others.

Of course, legal changes would do their best to protect those who did not wish to die. However, the experience of those countries where euthanasia has been accepted has led to concerns that the protections and safeguards would not prove sufficient. In particular, the experience in the Netherlands gives some support to those who fear a 'slippery slope'. There it is estimated that 1 in 40 deaths are now the result of assisted suicide or voluntary euthanasia. The category of 'unbearable suffering' has been interpreted widely to include many situations beyond terminal illness and physical distress. There is also evidence of doctors feeling free to give drugs with the intention of hastening the end of someone's life even without their consent.

Who does it?

The Dutch experience highlights that another important consideration in relation to euthanasia is its effect on the medical profession. If, even in a limited sense, people have a 'right to die' then it would seem to follow that someone must have a responsibility or duty to kill them, or at least to assist them in killing themselves. It may be that – as in the case of Dianne Pretty – the responsibility for this is taken up by relatives. That however is obviously not always free of problems, especially when the relatives benefit from the patient's death – as highlighted by the Schiavo case. More likely it is the medical profession who will be looked to for guidance, support and, where necessary, active participation in euthanasia. For many, that would represent a fundamental transformation (indeed perversion) of the doctor's calling. It would change the role and image of the medical profession, which would become a potential agent of death rather than of healing, comfort and life.

Conclusion

Undoubtedly one reason for the apparent growth in public support for euthanasia is the fear of a painful death, in which a person becomes increasingly dependent on others and perhaps has their life prolonged by medical intervention with the latest technology. We have already seen that a distinction can and should be made between 'euthanasia' and refusing excessive intervention. In the words of the nineteenth-century poet, 'Thou shalt not kill; but need'st not strive officiously to keep alive.' It is also important to recognize that dependency, however frustrating, is an essential feature of being human and is not inherently a sub-human or anti-human experience. There remains, however, the problem of pain. Is there no medical alternative to euthanasia here?

Since its foundation by Dame Cicely Saunders in the 1960s, the modern hospice movement has been at the forefront of providing an alternative response to the pain and suffering of the dying – that of palliative care. It recognizes that when, despite medical advances, doctors and nurses can no longer cure, they can nevertheless continue to care by providing pain relief and an environment of love and support for the dying. It is this alternative to euthanasia that has encouraged many religious people to continue to take their stand against euthanasia, and this has been seen most clearly in the response of Christian leaders and those of other faiths to recent changes to liberalize UK law in this area. Instead of supporting moves to accept euthanasia, most Christians have affirmed the view that in the face of pain, suffering and death the calling of Christians and of all humans made in the image of God is summed up as, 'Always to care, never to kill.'

More titles in the Lion Pocket Guide series:

A POCKET GUIDE TO THE BIBLE
Kevin O'Donnell

This small, very easy to use book combines an attractive design and concise text to give the reader an accessible way into the Bible. The book takes the reader step by step through the Bible, helping him or her to understand the key subjects and types of book it contains, and suggests passages of the Bible to begin reading.

'This is a marvel of scholarly compression and clarity; but it's more than that, because it helps the reader understand the Bible as a theological whole... The perfect gift for someone just beginning to read the Bible seriously, from teenage years onwards.'
Rowan Williams, Archbishop of Canterbury

ISBN: 0 7459 5313 7

A POCKET GUIDE TO SECTS & NEW RELIGIONS
Nigel Scotland

New religious movements are a subject of increasing interest
and relevance in our multi-cultural society. This handy little
book offers a concise overview of about 40 of the main sects
and new religious movements that have come to prominence
in the western world in recent years.

'This is a well-written, concise and reliable source for everyone not
wanting to get lost in the maze of new religious developments.'
The Methodist Recorder

ISBN: 0 7459 5159 7